What Tragedies Make

What Tragedies Make

A Novel

Elegy Lanier

For Maggie M.

Content guidance: This book contains depictions of child abuse and murder. Please read with care.

Chapter 1

A smile crept onto Kipp's face as she stopped in front of an old building with graffiti and peeling paint. Here in the East side of town, old abandoned houses were dotted in between empty lots of overgrown grass and juvenile trees. This one had caught her eye. It looked sturdier than some of the others that had roofs caving in. Made of what looked like stucco, the two-story home still had a few windows that hadn't been broken or cracked yet. There wasn't even that much graffiti on the outside. It was just begging to be explored.

The streets of Rundale, Colorado were near silent while Kipp had been walking around. Most of the small population was inside since it had been drizzling for most of the day. It was a relief for Kipp to walk around without her dog for once, having to spend the majority of the time making sure he didn't eat any dirt or knock her over trying to run after a bird. She opened the cracked front door and stepped through the waterlogged frame, tapping her foot on the ground to hear the echo.

The walls of the living room were covered in a blanket of moss-like growth, probably mold, and the scent of mildew drifted through the air. Kipp walked quietly through the building, letting her eyes drift over at each piece of graffiti she saw: words she could barely read through their outrageous fonts, a drawing of a skull, a small heart with S + D written in it, and a smiley face with paint dripping so it looked like its eyes were melting.

A sudden sound caused her to jump. Her attention was brought to the upstairs as she heard hushed voices travel through the halls.

She held her breath as she walked up the stairs, closer to the room the sounds were coming from and slowly leaning forward so that she could see into it. The blood in her veins turned to ice as she saw a group of men standing around, some in hoodies and dirty jeans, others in expensive-looking suits. A duffel bag filled with cash lay on the ground along with two packages covered in tape.

A tiny fleck of light bouncing off metal brought her attention to the numerous guns in the mens' hands. Some carried small pistols tucked into their pants or pockets, others casually held blunt-nosed handguns, waving them to make a point when they spoke.

"I'll be going to Boulder for a few months. Reed,

you better have the full amount for me when I get back," one of them said. Kipp's hand tightened around the handrail.

She had heard people talk about drug deals with things like cocaine and heroin and how they've gotten more common, but had never seen them herself, let alone something that looked this organized. The voices became more hushed, but Kipp could still make out a few words: the names "Smith" and "Franklin," and something about a workshop.

Kipp moved her now damp palms down the wooden rail, preparing to quietly walk back down the stairs. As soon as her foot pressed down on the stair behind her, the old wood let out a groan. The second she heard footsteps coming out of the room, she gave up on being quiet and sprinted for the door. Her face heated up from humiliation. She'd always thought that if she was in a dangerous situation like this she would stand her ground, or at least not go into a full panic, but here she was, running like a scared kid.

As she scrambled out of the house into the abnormally warm December air, a gunshot rang behind her. She only looked back once to see a man in a dark suit with murder in his eyes staring back at her.

. . .

Three months and one police report later, Kipp had started thinking about the incident a lot less. She never told her mom, figuring the chances of something like that happening again were next to nothing. It wasn't a good idea to spend time worrying over it, she'd got away after all.

Now, in March, Kipp's life had been busy with her lacrosse season. So far, she had lost count how many times she had made tea after getting home to help with her throat that was sore from constant yelling and quick breaths.

Today, her lacrosse coach was sick and the school hadn't been able to find anyone to step in, which ended up giving her the first day in a while she'd be free right after school.

"Hey, I don't have practice today. Do you guys want to finish up homework at my house?" she called into the nearly empty hall.

At this point in the day, there were only Kipp's close friends left in the hallway, save for a few stragglers walking to the door. Based on the way Kipp's shoes were able to slide across the floor with the dirt and dust, the floor could use a good cleaning. She hoisted her backpack onto her shoulders, grimacing as she closed her locker, the sticky remnants of a torn off sticker clinging to her fingers. This school had the visual appeal of an office building from the eighties.

Even Kipp's tanned olive skin took on an almost gray tone under the fluorescent lights.

"Sure! It's only like, a mile away, so do you guys want to walk?" asked Kipp's closest friend since sixth grade, Nikki. She pulled out the ear buds she always wore walking through the halls. You could hear the classic rock she was listening to from three feet away.

"Dude, it's so cold out!" their friend Luke whined, refusing to take a break from his constant complaining about the weather. "And I'll have to come back and get my car."

"Come on, it won't be that bad, even if it's a little chilly," their other friend Isabel assured in her usual bubbly tone as she pulled on her jacket.

"Fine. I guess I'll just suffer."

The group walked out of heavy glass doors of the school and down the gray stairs. Kipp immediately regretted leaving her flannel tied around her waist when the outdoors greeted her with a gust of frigid wind.

"Shit. Hold on, let me get my jacket."

The group waited as she set her backpack down and quickly pulled on the worn, burgundy shirt, shoes shifting uncomfortably on the concrete stairs.

"How's everyone feeling about the physics test?" Nikki asked when they started walking again, the bricks of the main school building drifting into the distance.

"I've studied all week, but I feel like I'm going to

forget everything," said Luke.

"I'm sure you'll do fine." Isabel gave a reassuring smile.

"Like you did on that precalc test?" Kipp teased.

"Hey! Give me some credit. I got a C plus on that," Luke said with a grin, earning laughs from the group. "You'd think they'd give us less work for senior year."

After a while of walking and talking, the nicely constructed public buildings and houses faded into rundown, dirty structures and warehouses. The sidewalk became broken in places, with weeds growing out from the cracks. This area had some issues with crime, but it was a much longer walk to avoid it. Besides, there were more and more neighborhoods like this one in Rundale these days. Crime rates everywhere were climbing, drugs taking off while incomes and population dropped. Not even five years ago, Rundale had been a city of 80,000. Now that number was under 70,000 and falling every year, leaving whole streets that felt abandoned.

Kipp didn't feel too unsafe in this neighborhood, though. The group had used this path many times, trusting their own judgment to keep them safe. Their parents tolerated it for the most part, as long as their kids carried self defense tools just in case. Nikki's mom was the one that convinced all the other parents to get each of them pepper spray.

"Everyone got their required weapons?" Luke

said, holding up his pepper spray can.

"Oh, shut up." Nikki smiled as she gave a light punch to Luke's shoulder.

The group turned their heads as they saw two men standing in an alleyway, muttering incomprehensibly. The smaller of the two fidgeted as he glanced over to the kids. The larger man made eye contact with Kipp from under his hood, or at least Kipp thought he did. It was hard to tell with how far the hood was pulled down. All she could make out was his jawline covered in patchy stubble.

Ignoring the two, Kipp and her friends continued walking, after all, they were a safe distance away. The smaller man skulked off in the opposite direction, back the way the kids had come.

The larger man, however, began walking behind the group. For a while, he kept his distance as if he was coincidentally going the same way as them. Kipp waited a while before she looked behind her, seeing that he was closer. Her friends continued walking, not sparing a glance behind them as they listened to Isabel share her thoughts on the new STEM teacher. When she was twelve, a man had followed her home from school. Ever since then, she never missed out on her surroundings.

A minute passed and Kipp continued to turn around every few seconds, heart beating a little faster each time. The man had sped up more and was now close enough that the grimace on his face was clear.

Kipp sighed and stopped walking, whipping around to face him.

"Why the hell are you following us?" she snapped, squinting as the wind whirled into her face. She could barely feel the cold.

The group stopped and turned around as well. The man didn't say anything, only stood in place with widened eyes, now fidgeting with his sleeve. Kipp pulled her taser out of her pocket, a present from her mother for her eighteenth birthday last week. Head tilted ever so slightly to the side, she raised her brows as if daring him to come closer. *Did he honestly think no one was going to notice him walking after us?*

The man looked from Kipp's taser to the rest of the kids, who had their hands in their pockets, ready to whip out their pepper spray. His hand tightened around something in his hoodie pocket. Eventually, he grunted an apology of some sort and finally walked off. A smirk tugged the corner of Kipp's mouth as she turned back around, heart still thrumming with adrenaline to prepare her for the confrontation.

"Nice job," said Nikki.

Isabel laughed nervously. "What do you think he wanted?"

"He might've been trying to rob us, and then thought it would be too much work when I said something," Kipp said, ignoring her thoughts rushing back to the men in the abandoned building from a few months ago.

"Wow, you're really learning a lot at that fake police internship," Nikki snickered.

"It's not fake, it's *unofficial.* There's a difference. Also, if I wasn't here, you guys might not have even seen that guy, so, you're welcome." Kipp batted her lashes with an innocent smile on her face.

"Dude, there's some weird people out here." Luke shook his head.

"There really are. One time, I saw this lady on a lawn chair in an alleyway putting vegetable oil on herself, and then she just went to sleep. I think she was trying to tan or something," said Kipp.

"With vegetable oil?" Isabel laughed.

"That's what the bottle looked like."

"She must've wanted some crispy skin," Luke commented, kicking a small rock across the pavement.

"Apparently," Kipp laughed. "Hey, do you guys want to do something Saturday? Maybe see a movie?"

"Sorry, I can't. I'm babysitting for some parents who are out of town this weekend," Isabel sighed. Kipp wasn't surprised. Isabel was too sweet to say no when parents in the neighborhood asked her to babysit, which happened often since they all loved her responsible nature.

"How old are the kids?" asked Nikki.

"It's only one kid, but she's a lot. She's six and thinks she knows everything. It's funny sometimes, but it also makes it hard to reason with her about why she needs to go to bed or why she can't do cartwheels until she throws up."

"Kids are so dumb. They all think they're super mature, and then try to boss you around all the time," said Luke.

"Yeah. When I turned ten I started hating the word 'playdate.' Every time my mom or someone would call it that I'd be like 'no, we're *hanging out!*'" Kipp put her hand to her chest, leaning back dramatically.

"Oh yeah, I did that too. Do you remember the first time we hung out together? We went to get ice cream and we both got so worked up over my mom and your aunt calling it a playdate?" Nikki asked.

"I remember that! You were kind of the saving grace for my social life," Kipp laughed, mulling over the memories: In sixth grade, she'd switched to a school in Rundale, since she was staying with her aunt there. She thought she'd make friends quickly, but even after two days of being in this town, she hadn't. It seemed all the other kids had already made their friend groups, most formed in elementary school, and weren't taking any late entries. It would have been a blow to anyone's ego going from table to table, each time seeing unwelcoming facial expressions and the occasional stereotypical, but still weighty "you can't sit here."

The third day of school though, things changed.

Kipp arrived in her first class right as the teacher was clapping her hands to get the children's attention.

"Everyone sit down! We're going to get started in a few minutes."

Kipp hurried to put her things in her locker and sat down at an empty table with her notebook and a pencil. The other tables soon filled up with happy children excited to talk with their friends. Kipp lowered her head, and began to doodle on the cover of her notebook, drowning out the chatter filling the room.

"Hey, can I sit here?"

A voice drew Kipp out of her bubble of focus. She looked up to see a girl holding a red composition notebook to her chest. She was wearing green shorts and a yellow T-shirt that didn't quite go together, her blonde hair fashioned into pigtails that reached just past her shoulders.

"Sure," Kipp replied, about to go back to doodling, assuming the girl only wanted to sit there because all the other tables were full.

"What's your name?" the girl asked. Kipp looked back up, for a split second wondering if she was even talking to her.

"Kipp. What's yours?" She closed her notebook.

"Nikki," the girl replied with a perky smile. "That's cool." She pointed to a small dinosaur Kipp had carved into her notebook.

"Thanks." Kipp looked Nikki up and down,

searching for something to start a conversation. "Do you like soccer?" she asked finally, seeing Nikki's over-the-calf socks covered in a soccer ball print.

"Yeah. I want to be a professional when I grow up. Do you play sports?"

"Not really."

"You should join one of the teams! There's so many. We have a *golf* team. I didn't even know that until yesterday. No offense if you like golf, but I think it's kind of stupid, especially to watch. I mean, it's *so slow*, it takes like ten minutes for someone to walk to where they hit the ball."

Kipp laughed for the first time she had started school. She knew right then that she and Nikki would end up being friends.

"Do you want to come over to my house after school?" Nikki had asked as she and Kipp walked to their next class. "I can call my mom with the school phone and ask if you can, but she'll probably want to meet your parents first."

The last bit of Nikki's sentence echoed around Kipp's head.

"My parents aren't there. My aunt is taking care of me."

"Oh, okay. Then, my parents will want to meet your aunt first," Nikki replied without missing a beat.

Kipp and Nikki happily went over to the phone right after lunch to call their guardians, and as the school day came to a close, Kipp's Aunt Nora and Nikki's mom parked their cars and waited for their children to walk out of the front doors. They stood behind the stairs talking to each other, oblivious to Kipp and Nikki peeking over the stairs at them, making sure not to talk and spoil their "spying." Kipp had suggested it as soon as she'd spotted her aunt, which wasn't very hard with the ends of her hair dyed a bright pink.

"Hi, are you Kipp's aunt?" a dark haired woman asked Nora.

"Yes, I am. You're Nikki's mom?"

"I am," the woman confirmed, standing up a bit straighter in her perfectly ironed pantsuit. "Katy Young. Nice to meet you..." Katy drew out the last letter, as she took a hand off her briefcase to stick out her hand.

"Nora Green," Nora replied, shaking it. "How long have you guys been in the area?"

"About fifteen years. How about you?"

"I've lived in Denver most of my life, but I moved here about three years ago. My brother Andre and his wife Roberta, Kipp's parents, lived in Colorado Springs. I'm taking care of her right now because they were in a car accident."

Kipp glanced at Nikki as they crouched down further, but Nikki didn't make eye contact.

"That's awful. I'm so sorry. Did her parents make it?"

"Andre didn't. Roberta is in a coma, but the doctors say she'll be okay."

"I'm so sorry about your brother. I hope Roberta ends up being all right."

"Me too," Nora sighed. She broke eye contact, checked her phone for a few seconds, and looked back up. "How's Nikki liking school?"

"She likes it so far, but she wasn't too happy when she heard there'd be more homework than elementary school," said Katy. "Is Kipp enjoying it so far?"

"She's told me about ten times how much she hates math, and how she doesn't want to read all the stuff in English, but she'll get used to it. I'm glad she's made some friends. She's always been a pretty social kid, but for the first couple days she said no one really wanted to talk to her," Nora said with a shrug.

"Mm-hmm. I was afraid Nikki would have that problem. She wasn't that outgoing in elementary school, but I think she's come out of her shell a little since then."

"That's good. Hey, did the girls decide what they wanted to do after school?"

"No. Maybe we could take them to get ice-cream?" Katy suggested. Nora followed her gaze toward the stairs. Her smile widened as she turned to the steps of the and saw Kipp and Nikki peering over the edge. Defeated, they both walked the rest of the way down the stairs. Upon reaching the bottom, they both gave their guardians a hug.

The ice cream shop thankfully had a short line. The walls were painted in light and dark blue stripes, and the small tables were a pastel green. The smell of sugar was potent in the air, and Kipp loved every bit of the small shop.

"I should come here more often!" Kipp exclaimed as she scooped up more with her spoon, a ring of chocolate already circling her mouth.

"Yeah!" said Nikki. "I come here about every other Friday. All their flavors are really good. Even the coffee one! Is that your favorite flavor?" Nikki pointed to Kipp's Rocky Road.

"Yeah. Is that yours?"

"No, cookie dough is my favorite, but I really felt like strawberry today, so I decided to do something different." She paused, putting her spoon down. "I'm sorry about your parents."

"It's okay. I still get to visit my mom sometimes."

"That's good. Tell me if you ever want to talk about it," said Nikki.

Kipp smiled at the offer. She hadn't met someone her age that had been this thoughtful.

Walking beside Nikki now, Kipp could see how her two dutch braids almost resembled those pigtails she wore all those years ago.

. . .

The old buildings soon transitioned back into more well kept grounds and tall trees.

Finally, they came to the winding, dirt driveway that led to Kipp's house. As they walked, dust swirled upward into light brown clouds that quickly dissipated into the air. Sunlight bounced off the oak tree leaves, shining down in patches along the path. In the distance stood an old brick house with dark burgundy shingles to match the dull reds and browns of the bricks. It was technically two stories, the second being the small, finished attic which also served as Kipp's bedroom.

"By the way, you guys might want to watch out for Milo, he's been hyper all day," said Kipp. "I took him for a shorter walk yesterday and he is not reacting well to it."

The friends walked up the cracked steps to the front door, stepping back as Kipp unlocked it. She jerked the metal handle to pull it open. Milo immediately came barreling toward the door, barking loudly. The Boerboel was far too big to fit beyond the door frame with the kids in the way, so he impatiently waited, tail swinging violently. Kipp shuffled forward, forcing Milo to move backward. Nikki was first through the door as soon as there was enough room to squeeze by.

"Back, Milo, back!" Kipp said firmly as Milo

tried to push past her to get to the trio putting their backpacks down by the door.

Kipp joined her friends at her kitchen table after shushing Milo a few times and giving him some head scratches when he quieted down.

"I see Milo's short walk came back to haunt you," Kipp's mother, Roberta Green, said with a good humored smile as she walked into the kitchen, meeting Kipp by the table for a hug.

"Yeah. At least he's not knocking stuff over like he did when he was a puppy."

It was difficult to imagine the house without Milo. That addition to the family was made a few years ago, when Nora came to their house with grievances of her landlord telling her that Milo barked too much and needed to go. Kipp and Roberta gladly took him in.

"You're home early," Kipp commented happily. Roberta towered over most people when wearing the four-inch heels she always wore to work, but with them off, Kipp was just barely taller.

"Yeah! I decided to cut my day short since we've run out of a few things. I thought we could also go over some of your application stuff later."

Being a real estate agent, Roberta was out of the house a lot. She was also a big fan of schedules, but once in a while she would abandon hers to take more time to be with her daughter.

"How was everyone's day?" she asked the kids.

A chorus of mildly enthusiastic responses filled

the room.

"It was pretty good," Kipp said, "but we all have a lot of homework. We have two more days until we have to turn in our history essays. Except for Luke, because apparently he didn't want to suffer through AP U.S. History with us." Kipp turned to Luke with her eyes widened in playful disapproval.

"Ah. Hopefully it won't be too miserable," Roberta said, patting Kipp's shoulder. "I've got to run to the grocery store, so call me if the house catches fire."

That earned some smiles from Kipp and her friends, but didn't stop the sigh from Kipp as she pulled out the stack of loose homework from her bag.

"I'm going to get the biggest case of senioritis when all my acceptances come in," said Luke. "At the very least, I'll have my safety school, so what's the point in putting in effort anymore? I bet I can get away with just not coming to school." He stretched his arms in the air before letting them drop to the table with a thud.

"Yeah, I don't know what the teachers expect. Almost every class I've had, one of them is like, 'Now, for all the seniors in the room, just because acceptances are coming in does not mean you get to stop trying.'" Kipp pitched her voice high in a mocking tone.

"It'll be a relief to not worry about getting in anymore," said Isabel.

"Says the smartest out of all of us," Nikki muttered. "If anyone has to worry it's Luke since he's planning on not even coming to school."

"First off, I said I could get away with it, not that I was going to do it. Second, how would colleges even know?"

"You do realize they get your final transcript, right?"

"Wait, really?" Luke leaned back in his chair, brows pinched together.

"Yep," said Nikki.

"I feel like teachers should've mentioned that when they were telling us not to slack off," said Kipp.

Everyone fell into silence as they started to work.

"Not to derail anyone's train of thought, but can you guys believe that guy tried to follow us like that?" Isabel spoke up.

"Yeah that was weird," said Nikki. "I feel like usually people doing drug deals and stuff in that area usually want to not interact with anyone above anything else."

"I'm glad I've started bringing that taser," said Kipp.

"Yeah, good day to have it." Nikki looked back at her laptop.

Kipp could barely focus on her work, though. She couldn't stop thinking about the possible connection between the people in the abandoned building and being followed. *The abandoned building thing was so long ago. I don't know how anyone would figure out who I was, and if they did, why wouldn't they do something sooner?*

What if it just took a long time to figure out who I was?

No. It's fine. There's a lot of weirdos in that area.

It's fine.

Chapter 2

The next day, Kipp awoke to an obnoxious xylophone sound. The tune was bouncing around the wooden walls and slanted ceiling of her room. She groaned, her first thought being that she forgot to turn off her alarm. *Shit. It's been so long since I forgot, too.*

But as her mind shook off the cloudiness from sleep, she realized the sound she was hearing was not her alarm.

Kipp grabbed her phone off the nightstand. The light from the screen eerily illuminated her room, which was otherwise enveloped in darkness thanks to the blackout curtains.

The time displayed on Kipp's lock screen read 8:34. She sat up, pushing the bright red and blue quilt off a little. The ringtone that woke her up was one she had picked specifically for when the captain of the local precinct, Captain Brumbly, called her. It was rare that he contacted her over the phone at all, but when he did, it was always something interesting. The ringtone stopped, replaced by the deep voice of Captain Brumbly as Kipp accepted the call.

"Hi, Kipp, how are you?"

"I'm good, how about you?" Kipp said, throwing the covers all the way off. Laundry left on the bed fell to the floor. She headed over to flip on the light, a small chandelier with lights that resembled flowers, which Kipp had brought over from her old house, unable to let go of her nostalgia.

"I'm well, thanks. I know it's a bit early, but we've just gotten the department involved in a big case that I think you'll find very interesting. If you're able to come down to the station, I can show you what we have so far."

"Yeah, I can be there in like fifteen minutes."

She threw on jeans and one of her nicer T-shirts and hurtled down the stairs to see her mother typing away on her computer at the kitchen table. Her deep chestnut-colored hair was mussed, and she still had on pajama pants as she clutched onto her coffee mug.

"Mom! Captain Brumbly said there's a case he wants to tell me about," Kipp announced. Roberta hadn't even finished rubbing the sleep from her eyes before Kipp dumped food into Milo's bowl and began stuffing a granola bar into her mouth. "I'm gonna ride my bike down there, I'll see you later!" Kipp said through a full mouth, crumbs spraying out onto the floor.

"All right, I love you, have fun!" Roberta called as her daughter grabbed her helmet and headed out the door.

"Love you too!"

While walking to her bike, which was propped up against the side of the house, Kipp pulled her hair into a low ponytail and snapped her helmet on. A few strands of honey-brown hair fluttered in her peripheral vision, looking almost golden in the light.

The precinct wasn't too far, and on days that were at least close to nice, Kipp would ride her bike. She favored biking to driving for many reasons: the environmental impact, the scenery, and of course the lack of anxiety that always came with driving. Today the sky was clear, save for a few wispy clouds high up in the atmosphere.

Kipp had met the captain many years before she became an unofficial intern for the precinct, when the captain was still a lieutenant and Kipp was twelve, living with her aunt Nora while her mom recovered from the car crash. It had been late September, and Kipp had been walking home from her bus stop with a spring in her step, oblivious to the figure trailing behind her. As she approached her aunt's apartment, which was situated in a rougher area that made most people extra paranoid, she looked behind her multiple times, but the man was still there, closer each time. She sped up, only to see that the man did the same. It didn't take her long to start running and screaming for the man to leave her alone. Right as she got to the apartment building doors, she saw the man had turned around and was walking in the other direction.

Nora was quick to notify the school and decided she would wait outside for her niece each day. She also eventually took Kipp down to a local martial arts studio in search of a self-defense class.

"We don't currently have any classes for children that are purely for self defense. If you want, could we enroll her in some beginner taekwondo classes?" the person at the front counter proposed. A man at the back of the lobby perked up even as the receptionist began his sentence.

"Hi, I'm sorry to interrupt, but I overheard you were thinking about getting some self-defense lessons. I'm Lieutenant Harold Brumbly." With a smile, he extended his hand for Nora to shake, and then to Kipp. "I've been doing some private lessons here for some time, and I could do some self-defense lessons with her a few times a week if you want," the man offered. "I'm volunteering here, so there's no need to pay. I'm usually available after four, but once in a while I'll have to stay later at the precinct."

Brumbly started with the very basics: particularly aiming for sensitive parts of the body, basic safety information like not being afraid to scream as loud as possible. He eventually let her progress to more hand to hand combat. It wasn't until her sophomore year that she was given more opportunities with her training.

On a cold, Saturday afternoon in early winter, Kipp had gone to the studio to train. A bead of sweat ran down her temple as she continued her boxing exercises with the punching bag in front of her. Being much taller now, she was finally able to reach the smaller bags that hung from the ceiling. As she put all of her stamina into punching the heavy bag in front of her, the rest of the room faded away. The only sounds she could hear were her fists connecting with the cloth and her own breath in her ears. As she pulled herself out of focus to get a sip of water, she noticed the lieutenant walking over to her.

"Hey, Lieutenant. What's up?" Kipp greeted.

"I got a promotion! It's *Captain* Brumbly now. " His exterior remained composed, but his eyes shone with excitement.

"Cool! Are you, like, the head of the whole department now?"

"Well, the precinct," he replied, a smile splitting his face. "I wanted to talk to you about something. I have decided that I won't be volunteering here anymore, but I *can* offer you some time with the police academy trainees if you're up to it."

Kipp's jaw nearly hit the floor. "I'm up to it! I'd love to!"

"All right then! Let me know what days you can

join in and I'll make it happen."

...

When Kipp arrived, she quickly jumped off the bike and locked it to the rack.

She entered the brick-staired building, then through a waiting room with tile floors that sparkled. The front desk worker smiled at her, pressing a button to let her into the back offices. Stopping at the captain's office door, Kipp pushed it open.

The dark wooden desk took up most of the room, the rest of the space filled by a bookshelf and metal cabinets. A small metal name plate reading *Capt. Harold Brumbly* sat on the edge. The middle-age man sitting at the desk looked up as the door opened. He was almost fifty with wrinkled almond-colored skin and small rimless glasses that he set on the table when Kipp walked in.

"Hi Kipp. You can have a seat." As usual, he wasted no time grabbing a blue folder from a drawer as Kipp sat down in the rolling office chair on the other side of the desk.

"So this case was originally being worked on in Boulder, but the Boulder police found a lead that a guy living over here is probably involved. His name is Anthony Hall. Apparently he ran a chemical company, got into some shady stuff, and then went off the radar. We think he could be the leader of this whole thing. You can look at that case file if you want. This one isn't confidential." He pushed the folder closer to her.

"Thanks." Kipp silently scanned the papers she was given, looking over the history of the company and what was dug up on Hall's childhood and parents. She stopped when she saw the picture that was paperclipped into the folder.

"Wait! I've seen this guy before! He was in the abandoned building that day! I think he was the one that said he was going to Boulder and wanted money when he got back."

"I hoped you'd recognize him. We're trying to set up an operation to catch him. We already have one person undercover currently, we'll probably send out a few more. I'll make sure to call you in if we find anyone that might've been in that building that day. I'm going to put the files from the report you made that day into the folder we have going for Hall and the drug case. Do you want a copy of the files about the case to take home?"

"Yeah, that would be good, thanks."

"All right," he said, drawing out his words as he stood up from the chair. "Let me go get that for you." He stepped out for a moment, leaving Kipp to check her phone and look around the office she had seen many times before. The same out of date computer, pen jar, and constant flurry of papers spread about the desk. This was the first time she'd been given an entire case file to take home.

"Here it is." The captain popped back in, presenting Kipp with a stack of papers secured with a large paperclip.

"So what do you guys know about Anthony Hall so far? Besides his chemical company thing?" Kipp asked, taking the papers.

"Well, he is quite the character. Apparently in Boulder, and in a few other counties, some known dealers have turned up dead. You know how you heard Hall saying something to someone called 'Reed'?"

"Yeah?" Kipp leaned forward.

"Well, someone named Jonathan Reed was one of the ones found dead. Shot point blank and then dumped in an alleyway like the others."

"Wow."

"Uh huh. The murders went unsolved for a while since it was a low priority to investigate a drug dealer's death, but Boulder PD started to notice that the type of gun used in all the murders was the same. The type of gun used wasn't extremely rare, but the bullets were unique. The casings found were red. We think it's meant to be a signature. A lot of the people who were found dead with the red casings around had evidence that they were planning on going somewhere or moving soon, like plane tickets and such in their homes or on their devices. That, or they had recently gone to the police for one reason or another. We think he's killing people who work for him that step out of line."

"Hm. How are you guys planning to move forward?"

"We're going to check records of drug dealers and their history around here to see if any high profile people fit the description of people he usually kills. We're also going to try to find out who Franklin and Smith are since you heard those mentioned. I'll update you on what's going on as we figure stuff out."

"Sounds good." She stood up.

"Hold on a second. If you've got time, I have an opportunity for you that I think you'll really like."

Kipp didn't sit back down, but she took a step toward the desk and folded her arms.

"I'm listening," she said with a grin.

"I'm conducting an interview today, and I might need some help from you. It's an interesting story of how we found out Hall was involved. One of our detectives was visiting this girl in Northeast Juvenile Center, or NJC. It's a training school, which is for high-level underage offenders. The detective and the girl would go on the computer every day she visited. This started a few months ago, I think. Long story short, the girl found evidence that Hall's old company could be involved with the drug ring."

"Is she saying she has more information now?"

"Yes. She claims to be getting notes from him,

but apparently none of the workers believed her, and now she refuses to talk to them about it."

"What's she in juvie for?" "Murder, I believe." The line's on Brumbly's head deepened. "She's getting released pretty soon."

"Really? They're just going to let her go after being convicted of murder?"

"She was convicted when she was twelve and she's seventeen now. It was technically legal to try her as an adult, but I guess the district attorney was feeling lenient, so she got time in the NJC instead."

"Do you know who she killed? And how?"

"I do not. When the detective gets back, you can see if she knows. I wouldn't recommend trying to ask the girl. I don't want to set her off. I've been told she was very reluctant to do the interview in the first place. Which is why I might need your help. If it doesn't seem like she's going to cooperate, I'll make up an excuse to leave the room and you, as a fellow teenager, can try to talk to her alone. Even if it doesn't come to that, I think it'll be a good experience for you."

"Yeah. Are there certain questions I should ask?" Kipp's smile was so wide, it hurt. She could've squealed in that moment.

"You should try to get to know her a little first. Don't just jump right into the questions. But the main points to hit are just why does she think Hall was the one sending them, why would he send them, and what do they say." He pushed himself out of his chair.

"Got it." Kipp cracked her knuckles as she walked with Brumbly to his car. *My first interrogation. And it's with a murderer! This is going to be fun.*

Chapter 3

The Northeast Juvenile Center was a white building with a flat roof, a lot of windows, and a heavy wood door with concrete steps leading up to it. The windows on the higher levels had metal screens instead of bars, but that didn't make the building any more inviting. Kipp's heart beat a bit faster as she prepared to come face to face with the murderer.

She walked inside with the captain, briefly stopping to go through the metal detector. The inside was just a few degrees away from being uncomfortably cold, and the peeling yellow walls didn't make it seem any warmer. Kipp and the captain began walking down a hallway toward the meeting rooms, breathing in the light scent of ammonia. A few posters were stuck to a corkboard on the wall: a schedule, a few motivational quotes, and a list of "community guidelines" that Kipp didn't bother to stop and read.

"Here's a recorder so that we can make sure everything is saved and documented. When we get in there, I'm going to turn it on, and begin the questions, and we can review the audio later if we need to go over specific details," said Brumbly.

Near the end of the hallway the captain stopped in front of a door and pushed it open. A girl in a navy hoodie and black sweatpants was sitting at one end of the gray plastic table. She was staring at the ground, a blank, yet sullen expression on her face.

"Hello," the girl said without looking up.

Her skin was pale, looking even more so in contrast with her dark brown hair. A thin scar started at her lower left cheekbone that twisted sideways, ending above her lips. She lifted her head, eyes moving to Kipp. Holding her own thin, delicate-looking wrist, she spoke again. "I presume you're Harold Brumbly?" she said dully, finally meeting the captain's eyes.

"Yes. And your name is...?"

"Morgan Toner." Her eyes trailed to Kipp again, a somewhat disapproving expression on her face.

"Nice to meet you, Morgan. This is Kipp, she's an intern with the Rundale PD. Is it okay if she sits in on the interview?"

"Yes," Morgan replied in a voice completely void of emotion.

"Well, I suppose we can get started, then," the captain said.

Looking into Morgan's eyes instilled a strange kind of anxiety in Kipp. Not exactly fear, more of an unease laced with a little something else. Pity, maybe.

Those cold blue eyes had an undertone of sadness in them… She continued to stare at the girl in front of her, analyzing every aspect of her expression in some attempt to break the surface of Morgan's shell. Kipp wondered how this girl had even gone about murdering someone. Whether it was disturbing or only confusing, she didn't know. The captain's voice broke through her thoughts.

"If you don't mind, I'd like to ask how you became involved with Hall, in order for him to want to send you notes."

Morgan's voice was soft and quiet as she stared at the table. "I did some research on a drug trafficking ring with Detective Carson and I discovered he was part of it."

Kipp squinted. *How could she do that locked in juvie?*

"Obviously Detective Carson used that information to further the investigation, so he does not like me very much," Morgan finished, raising her head a little.

"And what did the notes say?"

"They weren't very long, mostly vague threats, like 'stop looking while you still can.'"

"All right, and—"

"I'm sorry, could I have some water, please?" Morgan asked, rubbing the back of her neck.

"Yeah, I'll go get that. Do you need anything else?"

"No, just the water, thank you."

"I'll be right back." The captain stood up and left the room.

Kipp perked up, trying to catch Morgan's eye, but Morgan didn't look up, and instead began picking at her cuticles. Her shoulders were pressed tightly to her sides, and with no other sounds other than the air conditioning in the room, Kipp could hear her breathing was unsteady. *Maybe I'm more intimidating than I thought. She probably knows she can't scare me with her little Wednesday Addams act. Now's probably the time to get some info out of her.*

"So did he talk to you at all? Maybe about plans for something?" Kipp asked, leaning her elbows on the table.

Lips pursed, Morgan answered. "He never said anything to me in person. I can't be completely sure it was him in the first place."

"He didn't sign the notes or anything?"

"No."

"So this could just be a giant waste of time. Why did you want to do an interview?"

"I thought it would be helpful, especially if it is him."

"Then wh—"

"Shouldn't the police be the ones asking the questions?" Morgan snapped. Kipp narrowed her eyes, letting a moment of silence pass.

"Well, I'm working with them, aren't I?"

Morgan didn't answer, only lowered her head, picking even faster at her nails.

"We need this information! People could get hurt. I mean, maybe you don't care about that since you've killed someone before, but still, what do you have to lose?"

Morgan had stopped picking at her nails, and Kipp could see under the hair that had fallen in front of her face that her eyes had gone wide.

The captain returned promptly with the water.

"Here you go." He slid a paper cup over to Morgan, who took a tentative sip.

"Okay. In requesting to speak with an investigator, you mentioned—"

"I want to wait until Detective Carson is back," Morgan said quickly.

"She won't be here until tomorrow."

"I'll wait." Morgan tilted her chin up as she squeezed her wrist until her knuckles turned white.

"Okay then, I'll tell Detective Carson to visit you as soon as she gets here. Will you want to do an interview with her?"

"Maybe," Morgan mumbled, locking her eyes onto the table.

"We're going to leave now. Thank you for your time."

Kipp made her way up the corridor with the captain, curling her hands into fists and releasing them over and over again.

"She wasn't cooperative at *all*," said Kipp.

"Yeah, I think she might've been a little anxious. I'll get the detective to talk to her." Brumbly's perfect posture sagged a bit.

"Worth a try."

"I'll get something scheduled. You can try to watch again if you want."

"Sure. When will that be?"

"Maybe tomorrow."

Kipp would be ready. Morgan was difficult, but Kipp wouldn't let her walk away without giving at least a *little* valuable information, even if it was that she was lying about the notes.

After being escorted back to her dorm on the other side of the building, Morgan remained curled up on the edge of her bed for a long while after the captain and his intern left. She had been through a number of rooms since she was there, moving from unit to unit as she grew up. This one was the largest she had been given, with a twin bed and desk for her remaining few weeks in the training school. Most rooms had two people in them, but since Morgan had a history of getting little to no sleep when sharing a room, she was given her own. The bed had white sheets, a single pillow and a light blue throw blanket, which Morgan had wrapped around herself.

Detective Amelia Carson had been gone for a couple days, but at least she was supposed to come back early tomorrow morning. The detective had helped her with so much since Morgan met her a year ago. The NJC had classes on certain trades like welding, but at around age fourteen, Morgan had yearned for something else. She begged any worker she saw to bring her something else to do. A book on sociology, a few minutes on a computer to look at an article or a Khan Academy course, *anything* else. When she was fifteen, she even suggested talking to a local detective to learn about criminal justice. Many of the workers seemed amused by her persistence, others kindly explained that she would not get that opportunity here, especially with no one to pay for a tutor or textbook.

Then, one day last year, a worker pulled her aside to tell her that an actual detective had offered to talk to her once a week, saving her one less trade class.

After her session of online school, Morgan was left to wait in a room while someone went to bring in the detective. Eventually, a woman walked through the door. Her hair was pulled into a messy braid that contrasted with her neatly pressed blazer and jeans.

"I'm Detective Amelia Carson," she said, extending her hand.

"Nice to meet you, Detective. My name is Morgan. I can't believe they actually let me talk to someone!" Morgan balled up her hands in excitement.

The detective smiled. "Funny story about that, actually. I don't think they were going to, but somehow word got around to me that someone here really wanted to learn about criminal justice instead of trade classes, so I said I'd come down here and talk to them about it. I offered to do it for everyone in the facility, and they said they'll have me do a speech some other day, so you might be hearing some of this twice, but if you or any other people here want to go more in depth, I am totally willing to come back. I would say we could do something during visiting hours, but I don't want to get in the way of any family coming to visit or anything."

"That's okay. I don't think I'll have anyone coming to visit."

"Oh." Detective Carson paused as if she was about to ask why, but stopped herself. "Well, then, I'll have to start coming by," she said instead. "I've never done any teaching before, so I don't really know what I should start with. Did you have any specific questions?"

"I have a few."

Morgan asked about the investigation process, people's different roles when working on a case, how evidence is shown in court, and anything else she could think of. She hoped the detective wouldn't be caught off-guard by her excitement. It felt like she had forgotten how to have a normal conversation. After an hour of talking, Morgan had to go on to another activity.

"It was nice to meet you." Morgan beamed when

the detective stood up to leave.

"It was nice to meet you, too. I'll definitely make sure to come back soon."

Amelia continued to visit over the following months, coming more and more frequently. Morgan didn't interact with the other kids very much, so being able to talk to Amelia helped her feel like she wasn't going insane. The detective was easy to talk to, with a constant smile and soothing voice. It was one of the few times she felt seen, rather than a near invisible object that needed to be guided around the facility. She often wondered if there were kids her age outside the facility who felt that way, with no one to talk to. There probably were. Certainly not the girl from the interview, though. Kipp seemed too bright to miss.

Morgan pulled her knees closer to her chest, only wanting the next day to come sooner.

...

The next day, Kipp met with Nikki and Luke at their favorite cafe, the Cafe Roxy, for breakfast. They gathered at the booth they always sat at, not bothering to look at the menus.

"Where's Isabel?" asked Kipp.

"She said she was going to be a few minutes late," Luke said, not looking up from where he was sketching on a napkin. Just as their waiter arrived with some water, the door to the cafe burst open.

"Guys. Guess what? I got into the University of California Irvine!" Isabel announced as she skipped over to the table, her blunt bangs swishing across her forehead.

"That's awesome!" Kipp exclaimed.

"Congrats!" said Luke.

"That was the one you were hoping for, right?" asked Nikki.

"Yeah! They have a good bio program, and now I get to go to California. Maybe I can learn to surf. Has anyone else gotten acceptances yet?" asked Isabel.

"I got into the University of Colorado," said Kipp. "The Denver one. I got into a few safeties too, but I think I'm going to go with Colorado."

"Oh cool," said Nikki. "I need to actually figure out what I want to major in. I'll probably do business. I'm thinking about becoming an operations research analyst or something. I think they make pretty good pay. So far, I've heard from some of my safety schools, but not from my top one yet."

"Same. I just want to know already," Luke groaned as he fiddled with his fork. "I really want NC State because the design program is really good."

"You're going to have a hell of a time there," Nikki laughed.

"What do you mean?"

"Well, for starters, you always wear giant sweaters. It's super humid down there."

"Eh, I'll be fine." Luke dismissed the concern with a flick of his wrist.

As her friends talked, Kipp found herself staring into her plate, the sights and sounds around her melting away as she considered the events of yesterday. No matter how hard she tried, she couldn't bring herself to think of that girl as unlikable. Annoying, and mildly infuriating, yes, but not completely unlikable. Maybe it was her empathy acting up. She wouldn't be that friendly either if she was locked up in there. But empathy didn't explain why she'd found it so hard to look away from her eyes.

"What's everyone going to do for the last bit of the weekend?" Luke asked.

"I'm going rock wall climbing with my parents. We're going to that indoor one in Denver," said Nikki.

"Nice. What about you guys?" Luke asked, turning to the rest of the table. Isabel glanced at Kipp before saying,

"I'm not doing much, just getting some new bedding for my guinea pig."

Kipp eventually noticed everyone looking at her, waiting for an answer.

"Oh," she said, snapping out of her daze, "yeah, I'm going to stay at my place, maybe go for a hike or something." She shoveled a bite of her eggs into her mouth.

"You got anything going on with the police?" Luke asked.

"Yeah, actually. Captain Brumbly told me about this new case the department is getting involved in." She leaned in a bit and lowered her voice to explain the Hall case, and eventually the interview with Morgan. "...She talked a little bit, but then she was like, 'I don't want to do this anymore!' The captain said I could watch another interview with her, but she didn't say she'd definitely do another interview, so it might not happen."

"Let's hope she agrees to it," Nikki laughed. "What was it like meeting a killer?"

"I dunno," Kipp said through her bite of eggs. "It sort of makes you feel uneasy knowing that a person sitting feet away from you has murdered someone. The girl herself is pretty normal-seeming, even though she's not all that warm with people."

"That sounds about right. You know, with her being a murderer and all," Nikki said with another laugh, this one with an audible edge to it.

"That sounds scary. They just let you sit in a room with her?" Isabel interlaced her fingers on the table.

"I mean, it's not like she was going to do anything. They don't have access to weapons there, and there was no way she was going to be able to overpower me *and* the captain."

"Why did she only want to talk to that one detective?" asked Luke.

"I don't know, I guess she's just *super* shy." Kipp pressed her shoulders to her sides as she shifted around, tucking her chin into her chest. Her friends laughed at her sarcastic display.

"Ooh, let me just shyly slit this person's throat." Luke wheezed, twirling a butter knife around.

Kipp laughed along, but she knew her sarcasm was misplaced. Morgan *was* shy, even if it was padded by hostility.

It only made Kipp want to see what was underneath it more.

That same day, at the training school, Detective Carson finally arrived in Rundale.

"Hi Morgan," she said as she walked into the doorway of Morgan's room.

"Hi." Morgan immediately stood up, an instinctual smile on her face. The skin under the detective's eyes looked just a bit darker than usual, but her pupils still had their animated shine.

"I heard you had an interview with the police captain that didn't go so well," she said, crossing her arms.

"The guards were talking about a case involving Anthony Hall. I wanted to tell them about the notes I got, since maybe they'd take them more seriously now. They started asking me a bunch of questions, but they were going so fast and I could barely answer them. They got more aggressive when I couldn't answer stuff, and eventually I just stopped talking because I wanted them to go away." Morgan took in a breath. She sat back down on her bed. "I was trying to calm down after that, but they took me into a room and said I needed to do an interview. Captain Brumbly wasn't mean or anything, but I said I wanted to wait for you to get back and do an interview with you."

"That's okay. I'm sorry that was so overwhelming, but it's great someone's finally looking into the notes. We can try the interview again tomorrow. Just relax until then. You have your session with the psychiatrist soon, right? I heard they got a new one."

"The last one retired. He wasn't fun to talk to, but at least I was familiar with him."

"I'm sure this one will be okay. If you really don't like whoever it is, I'm sure I can work something out with the facility. And if I can't, you only have about a month left in here."

A worker knocked on the open door. "Morgan, it's time for your appointment with Dr. Pearce."

"I can walk her over there," said Amelia. The worker nodded and walked away.

Detective Carson had walked with Morgan a few times before, so she knew where to stop along the hallway, although the name on the door had been taken off. "I'll see you for the interview. If you want to talk afterward, just let me know. Have a good session."

Morgan knocked on the door, waiting until she heard a "come in" from the other side. She started wringing her hands even before she sat down.

"Have a seat and we'll get started. You're Morgan Toner, right?" the woman asked. Morgan flicked her gaze away, biting the inside of her cheek. The woman looked unfamiliar, but her *voice*... "Can you answer me?" the psychiatrist prompted. Morgan jerkily snapped her head to face the psychiatrist and nodded. That voice. It was so eerily similar to her mother's.

Keeping her eyes glued to the woman in front of her, Morgan repeated in her head like a mantra that obviously this woman wasn't her mother, that she had no reason to worry.

"Okay," the woman continued, "and can you tell me why you're here?"

Morgan broke her gaze again, breaths quickening. "I—" Her heart felt like it was ready to break out of her rib cage. Suddenly, it felt as if her entire chest had collapsed. She couldn't breathe. She tried focusing on the psychology books on the shelf, or the stress toys lined up on the desk, but it didn't help.

Morgan tried to stand up only to topple back into the chair. The psychiatrist rushed around the desk, holding Morgan in place as she tried to stand up again.

"You're having a panic attack. I need you to try to take some deep breaths, okay?"

Morgan sucked in half a breath, sputtering it out a second later. "I can't—"

"Yes you can," the woman said calmly. "Breathe in." She waited until Morgan shakily inhaled before continuing. "Breathe out."

After Morgan had calmed down a bit, the remainder of her session was taken up by the psychiatrist prodding to figure out what made her so upset. Morgan never gave a clear answer. After that, she was taken back to her dorm. She crawled into bed, pulling the blanket over her entire body and curling into a ball to cry.

She could remember crying at her fifth birthday party. Right after her mother slapped her for taking a barrette out of her hair because it was painfully tugging some tangled strands. But there were worse memories...

She remembered her alarm going off, the shrill beeping calling her to turn it off.

The sun had not yet spread its rays over the sky, and her room was shrouded in shadow, making the pink walls appear almost gray. Footsteps began stomping up the stairs, rattling the small porcelain sheep on her shelf. Before Morgan could hush the insistent noise of the alarm, her bedroom door flew open.

"Morgan Sadie Toner! Get up, right now!"

Morgan immediately scrambled out of bed, like a bug being exterminated from its hideout.

"I set an alarm—"

"I don't care. You should be up by now." Her mother grabbed her arm with an iron grip, nails digging deep into her skin as she dragged her into the bathroom.

"I need time to make sure you look presentable. Hold *still.*" Her mother began removing the curlers from Morgan's hair, leaving it in large ringlets like a doll's. After the curls have cascaded halfway down Morgan's back, her mother grabbed a comb and started tugging through them mercilessly, disregarding her daughter's grimace. Morgan took deep breaths, focusing on her own face in the mirror with gloomy blue eyes and almost sickly porcelain skin, trying her very best not to let out a whimper of pain.

Her mother fashioned her hair into a ponytail. After putting a minimal amount of makeup on her daughter, covering the large bruise on her chin, Morgan's mother gave her a white half-sleeved dress with yellow flowers embroidered on, something that would surely leave her shivering in the heavily air conditioned classrooms. The cold air always seemed to go straight to her bones.

Morgan walked downstairs with her backpack, entering the kitchen with ramrod straight posture. She knew most ten-year-olds had a lot more energy than her, which only made it harder for her to make friends. But she was still wrapped in the disguise of a picture perfect daughter in every way, except for her nonexistent smile.

"Morgan, you're late coming down. Go help your mother with breakfast," Morgan's father barked at her. She set her bag down by the table and went to help her mother at the stove.

"Here. Finish the eggs, but don't get your dress dirty," her mother said, thrusting the spatula at her. Morgan took it, and began to do as she was told.

Every morning was the same. Morgan would wake up, her mother would make sure she looked "presentable." After that, she was badgered to make breakfast and set the table.

Sleeping in was unheard of for Morgan, and there was never a break from domestic chores. Scrubbing the kitchen floor, doing laundry, folding linens and clothes, and the list went on. Even when there was seemingly nothing more to be done, her parents would insist that another round of dusting or scrubbing was needed. When she was very young, she found it a little odd that her parents never helped, but when she heard her mother talking with a friend about how nice it was to basically have a live-in maid, it made a little more sense. "With all the energy and money that went into raising her, the least she could do is give us some opportunity to relax," her mother had said, taking a sip of coffee through upturned lips.

Morgan set the table quickly, scolded by her parents when a plate clattered. Most of the food was gone before they gave Morgan permission to take some of it. She shoved a piece of toast in her mouth to eat while she was walking.

The facility would serve dinner soon, and Morgan would have to wipe her eyes and get out from under the blanket. But until that knock came at her door, she'd stay in bed, listening to her own breaths.

Chapter 4

Sparse trees came and went from the view of the passenger window. Kipp's eyelids were threatening to droop as the squad car slowly swayed with the turns it made.

There were only two experiences Kipp had while tagging along on patrol. There would either be something interesting going on and she'd watch the officers deal with the situation, or she would be asleep by the time they arrived back at the precinct.

"Looks like things might be a little boring today," said the officer next to her, who Kipp only knew as Jordan. "Or maybe interesting if you find the elderly calling the cops on kids smoking near their house funny. It happened once yesterday, and *twice* already today. I think two of the calls were from some old lady that has nothing better to do than sit at her window and try to get kids in trouble. On one of the calls the kids weren't even smoking. They were these little kids trying to see who could make the biggest cloud by blowing out hot air so the cold made it into steam."

"Wow," Kipp laughed. "There are two types of old people here: the ones that let everyone pet their dogs and give out massive candy bars on Halloween, and the ones that do stuff like that." She sat up straighter as the radio came on.

"Unit 558, we have a possible 10-62 in progress at 4790 Gulf Street. Unit 785 will be assigned backup."

Jordan pressed a button on his radio. "Ten four, unit 558 en route."

"Unit 785 is en route for backup," a voice on the radio responded.

"Looks like we'll have some action today after all." He switched on the car's siren and lights as it made a sharp turn onto a side street, almost causing his main source of energy, his second Diet Coke of the day, to spill. Zooming around with the siren on always made Kipp giddy with adrenaline.

As they drove, the operator continued. "The caller is a sixty-two-year-old woman, Catherine Lovett. She lives alone and says she saw a car she'd never seen before pulling up near the house. She saw one person get out and walk around to the back."

The car came to a stop at a white house where the officer and Kipp exited and approached the door to Catherine Lovett's house.

Jordan rapped twice on the door. "Police."

The door was opened by a gray-haired woman

with deep lines in her forehead and thin, pursed lips.

"Ma'am, you called about a burglar at your neighbor's house?"

"Yes. I saw a car I didn't recognize parked near the house and then someone got out and walked to the back of the house."

"Was the person carrying anything? Maybe a weapon?"

"He had a wrench, or a hammer, or something like that."

"Are your neighbors away?"

"Yes, they're out of town. Have been for a few days."

As Jordan continued questions, another squad car made its way down the street, parking in front of the house across from Catherine's.

"Thank you for your time, we'll let you know if we find anything," Jordan concluded.

He and Kipp walked over to the squad car that had pulled up a few seconds ago, joining the other officer in looking around the outside of the house.

"What'd she say?" the second officer asked, resting a hand on her belt as the sun reflected off her slicked back bun.

"The only visible weapon the suspect had was a blunt object that looked like a hammer or a wrench. The owners are away. Kipp, you can wait here."

Kipp leaned against the front of the car, watching as both officers tried the door. They circled to the back of the house after they found it locked. She glanced at her cuticles, which had a few small spots of blood on them from being picked at when she was bored. *What're the chances this guy is related to Hall? Probably not. But it kind of seems like there's been more reports about stuff lately. Like the two loitering reports from last week.*

It's probably a coincidence.

She looked around the neighborhood of closely-spaced houses. Most were made of wood with small porches and little decorations in the front yards like flowers or gnomes.

Movement near one of the houses caught Kipp's eye: something that looked like a person ran into the yard next to the house being investigated. She stared for a moment, wondering if it was just a dog or something. It couldn't hurt to just peek into the backyard.

Kipp walked through the overgrown grass to the short gate blocking off the yard, peering over. She heard what sounded like a door quietly close. After hoisting herself over the fence, Kipp jogged to the back door, looking into the home's windows on the way. She didn't see anything, but still approached the door. It was cracked open. Kipp didn't want to get in trouble for trespassing, but if there was someone in there, she'd always regret being too scared to check.

She stepped inside the small, dimly lit home. The hardwood floors looked pretty old. Hopefully they wouldn't squeak the second she put weight on them. The door opened into the living room where a couch and TV sat next to a large bookshelf filled with knicknacks.

Dread began to pool in Kipp's stomach as she heard a small noise from farther in the house. *Is there someone home? Or did someone break in?* She slowly scanned the living room using the light provided by the windows, creeping closer to where she heard the noise.

It had come from what looked like a bedroom. The door was halfway open, and Kipp thought she could see a figure through the crack between the door and the wall. Clenching her hands in fists, she exhaled shakily, eyes darting around for anything she could use as a weapon. There was nothing in sight that she could get to without making noise.

After standing there for a moment, Kipp took a deep breath and ran at the door.

She crashed into it with her shoulder with as much force as she could. The man hiding behind the door yelped as he was slammed against the wall. He stumbled out from behind the door, but quickly got his bearings and snatched a lamp off the nightstand behind him.

"Jordan!" Kipp yelled, hoping the officers could hear. The man charged toward Kipp, pitching the lamp at her. She swiftly dodged it as the intruder tried to run past her. Sliding to the side, Kipp landed a hard kick at the man's shin. He stumbled, giving Kipp the opportunity to land another kick to his stomach. He sputtered out a few coughs, but quickly reeled his fist back for a punch.

Pain shot like fireworks across Kipp's jaw as the blow connected. She grunted in response, but threw her own punch which she felt land square in the middle of the man's face.

He turned to make a break for the door, but before he could get there, Kipp threw herself at him, latching onto his neck with both arms. He spun around in circles, aggressively running Kipp into walls in a desperate attempt to throw her off, but she managed to hold on. She could tell the man was getting weaker due to the lack of air. Just then, she heard Jordan's faint voice from outside.

"Kipp? Where are you?"

"There's someone in here!" Kipp screamed.

The man continued to struggle, almost throwing Kipp off when he turned, slamming her against a door frame. Finally, Jordan and the other officer burst through the back door and drew their guns on the man. After he had lifted his hands up, Kipp let go of his neck and went to stand beside Jordan. The man was cuffed and escorted to the other officer's car.

"You're lucky that guy didn't have a weapon and was just interested in getting away," said Jordan. Kipp nodded in half-hearted agreement. "You should've told us you saw him go in there, though. But I have to say, that was pretty impressive."

Kipp smiled. "I didn't want to go get you and have him be gone by the time you guys got there."

"How about you call me if anything like this happens again? But call me *before* you trespass on someone's property." Jordan laughed.

"Will do," said Kipp. "He didn't look like he had stolen a bunch of stuff. Was it in his pockets or something?"

"He had some cash in his pockets, but he didn't take anything else. There were some pretty nice headphones and a laptop that were left in the house. We did find a few small bags of white powder on a desk. We're sending it for testing, but I'm pretty sure it was coke. I think what might've happened is the guy that broke in was a dealer and someone owed him money."

Kipp hummed in agreement. *So this really could be connected to Hall.*

There were reporters knocking on Kipp's door not even two hours after she got home.

"Over the past few weeks, there have been a number of home burglaries in East Rundale. I'm here with eighteen-year-old Kipp Green, who just this afternoon stopped a burglar from fleeing the police. Kipp, can you tell us what was going through your mind?"

Kipp put on a smile as the reporter thrust the microphone at her. "Uh, I guess I was just thinking that since I was there, and the police didn't know he was hiding in another house, that he'd probably get away if I didn't do something."

"Weren't you afraid?"

"A little bit, I guess. But he didn't draw a weapon on me or anything."

"What prepared you to be so brave?"

"I mean, I've taken some self-defense classes and I've worked with the police department some, but that's about it."

"How do you feel now that you're a hero?" the reporter prompted.

The microphone was outstretched to Kipp as she laughed in surprise.

"Good, I guess. I didn't really think I'd be considered a *hero* for this. I'm glad to help out, though."

"Do you think you'll want to go into criminal justice when you're older?"

"Yeah, that's what I'm planning on."

"Alrighty then! Thank you for your time."

The camera previously pointed at her was lowered as the crew walked back to their van.

Roberta arrived home about thirty minutes later as Kipp was putting ice on some of her new bruises.

"Mom, a news station came over here to talk to me about stopping a burglar with Jordan today,"

Kipp said as soon as her mother walked through the door.

"Oh wow! What happened that made them want to talk to you? Did something crazy happen?"

"I saw the burglar go into another house and stopped him from getting away."

Roberta's eyes widened, her tone becoming much more serious. "You didn't get hurt did you?"

"I mean, I was on the guy's back, so he slammed me into some walls, but nothing hurts too bad."

"Oh my God. Was Jordan even there when that happened?"

"He got there pretty quickly. I know I shouldn't have gone into the house. Jordan said I can call him next time I see something weird."

"Yes, please do. I don't want you getting hurt or in trouble for something like that."

The next time she went to the precinct, Kipp found the captain waiting for her with crossed arms. Her confidence carried her over to him without an ounce of reluctance.

"I heard that *someone* got into a brawl with a burglar," he said.

Kipp couldn't help but smile, even though the captain had made his lips into a disapproving flat line. "You could have been hurt or even killed. I taught you self-defense so you could *defend* yourself from attacks that you couldn't get away from. And

I let you go on these ride-alongs so you can learn about the job, not so you could play hero and run headfirst into dangerous situations."

"But I stopped him, didn't I?" Kipp countered. The captain scoffed, but Kipp could see a smile flicker across his face.

"Just promise me you won't hurt yourself, okay? You've got a lot of life ahead of you. And you can always join the force later on," the captain pointed out.

"I guess."

...

The day after going on patrol with Officer Jordan, Kipp received a call from the captain letting her know that Morgan had agreed to another interview. The detective leading it would meet her outside the training school right after Kipp finished lacrosse.

Kipp spent some time in the bathroom wiping sweat off her face and re-tying her hair before changing out of her practice clothes. She drove to the center and met a dark-haired woman with bright red rectangle glasses at the doors.

"Are you Kipp?" the woman asked.

"Yeah."

"I'm Detective Amelia Carson." She raised her ID off her shirt. "Before we go in, if you want it, I have a packet with some information on Morgan.

It has some basic info if you want to read through it. I think it'll help you understand her a bit better. You don't have to look at it now, but I've always found having a solid background on people makes interviews and interrogations go smoother." The detective extended her hand, offering Kipp a manilla folder.

"Thanks, I'll definitely take a look at it. Does it say who she killed?" Kipp let out a small laugh, but stopped as she saw the detective looked far from amused.

"It has the police report and some other old documents. I trust you know enough to not go around sharing that information."

Kipp felt a twinge of embarrassment. She probably shouldn't have laughed.

Together, they walked inside.

All the while walking to Morgan's room, Kipp gave herself a pep talk. *Be calm and collected. Do not show any emotion. It'll only give Toner an edge, and make the detective think less of you. Just calm down.*

They approached Morgan's dorm room and entered through the plexiglass door.

"Hi Morgan, we're here to try that interview again," the detective greeted, voice turning much softer.

"Hi Detective," Morgan said back, her face much brighter than the first time Kipp saw her. "Kipp." She nodded to the less than happy girl beside Detective

Carson.

"Hey," Kipp said, straight-faced. *Come on. Be more serious. And more confident. You're strong, you're smart, you shouldn't be this jittery—* Her thoughts were interrupted as a worker walked in holding two stools. "I hope you're ready to actually do a full interview this time," Kipp managed. The detective looked at her with an expressionless face, although it still looked kind of like a glare. They both sat down.

"Are you okay to go ahead and get started?" Detective Carson asked. "Yes," Morgan answered.

Carson pulled out her phone and began a recording. "Okay, then let's start. You've mentioned the notes to me before, but just to have it on the recording, can you recall how you got involved with the Anthony Hall case and the details of the notes you were sent?"

Then Morgan began to explain.

A few months ago, she'd seen a guard reading a local newspaper. There was an article about the police's investigation into a possible drug trafficking network on the cover. The main drug being discussed was cocaine laced with an extremely addictive unknown substance. Most of what Morgan had heard about Rundale boiled down to it being a boring small town with a relatively low crime rate that was mostly made up of petty crimes. She asked if she could read it when the guard was finished and ended up taking it back to her room. Even after skimming the article, she knew she had to know more. She asked Amelia if she knew a lot about the case. Amelia was one of the lead detectives on it, so she was happy to answer any questions that Morgan had.

When the detective visited her, Morgan would investigate using an old computer that Amelia brought. She went onto a few dark web sites that she'd heard about from another kid in the facility. The laced cocaine was apparently being referred to as 'unicorn dust'. Most of what was being posted about it came from the same anonymous user. The detective took it back to the department and they eventually found the IP address and were able to get the name of the device owner. It was an elderly woman, but apparently her computer had been stolen. The main suspect was an ex-convict named Kevin M. Brooks.

Brooks had been arrested on suspicion of drug trafficking, and once convicted for drug possession. It was said the police had long suspected he was part of something larger.

"Do you know anything about Kevin Brooks?" Morgan had asked Amelia.

"I've heard of him, but I wasn't in charge of his case or anything. But, I work with this guy, Davey Ackerman, a lot, and he was on the case. He works in forensics now, but he'll still be able to help us out."

"Do you think you could get me a case file on him?"

"Sure. I'll bring a paper copy tomorrow."

The next day, Amelia sat next to Morgan in the visiting room as she looked through the file. Previously, Brooks worked for a chemical company called G.H. Chemical that was no longer in operation. She found the company's old website on the Internet Archive, learning that the head of the company was a man named Anthony Hall, who ran the company after it was passed down to him by his father. Morgan did a quick search to try and find out why the company discontinued its operations. From the sources she found, it seemed as if Anthony Hall simply disbanded his employees and shut the company down himself. The seemingly hasty press statement that was given said that new EPA policies were making it impossible for them to stay open.

"That's weird. It looks like in the last few years there's only been minor policy changes that have to do with industrial cleaning solutions," Morgan thought out loud. The detective leaned closer to the screen.

"Yeah, that's interesting. Let's try to find something else on Anthony Hall."

After a few minutes of frustrating searching that brought up nothing, Morgan came across a news article from an obscure website. It detailed that G.H. Chemical received unmarked cardboard boxes every few days, all from cleaning service vans rather than some sort of official company truck. The author seemed to think Hall was using some sort of chemical that went against local environmental protection laws, but Morgan and the detective had other ideas.

"Do you think this is enough to look into Hall?"

"Yeah, I do. I think this could actually be a pretty good lead," said Amelia.

Morgan was always relieved to be back in her room. She walked in ready to collapse on the bed, but the small envelope stopped her. She picked it up. There was no address, no name, and no stamp on the outside. Sliding her nail under the fold, she ripped it open. There was a folded paper tucked inside. Morgan clenched her jaw when she unfolded it. There was only a single sentence written in what looked like black marker.

Tupq mppljoh xijmf zpv tujmm dbo.

Morgan squinted. "What?" she whispered. After crossing out the possibility of the writing being in another language, she considered it might be a code. She carefully ripped out a page of a coloring book she had left on the desk, making two scraggly circles where she wrote out the alphabet on the edge of both to make a makeshift decoder. Hoping it was a simple Caesar cipher, she started with matching a to z, b to y and so on to see if it turned one of the shorter groups of letters into a word. That yielded nothing, but she kept trying. It looked like shifting it forward by one was the solution when it revealed the first three letter group as 'you'. She went through the rest of the words and finally, the message was revealed: 'Stop looking while you still can.'

Morgan's eyes widened to the size of saucers.

Although the note concerned her at first, and the drug ring investigation briefly flew through her thoughts, she decided it was probably a prank, or maybe a threat from one of the other kids. Just a few days ago, some of them had threatened her after she'd seen them with a baggie of weed. Not wanting to bother the guards with something that could very well be nothing of concern, she threw it away and continued to research with Amelia about the case.

A few days later, another letter arrived, and in the same marker, it read:

Ck cuarjt'z cgtz gteutk zu mkz naxz, cuarj ck, Suxmgt Ygjok Zutkx ul Murjkt, Iuruxgju?

This time, it was shifted by six, and it said: 'We wouldn't want anyone to get hurt, would we, Morgan Sadie Toner of Golden, Colorado?'

Her research with the drug ring really came to mind this time. But how in the world could anyone know she was involved?

At the first opportunity she had, she showed the guard the note.

"Have you received any other notes like this?" the guard, a man Morgan had heard workers call Jay, asked.

Morgan reluctantly took in a breath to speak. "There was one on my bed a few days ago. That one was also in a Caesar cipher. It said 'stop looking while you still can,' but I thought it might be a prank or something, and I didn't want to bother anyone, so I threw it away."

"You threw it away," Jay repeated, scratching his receding hairline.

"Yes." Morgan lowered her head. It was a stupid decision. "When Detective Carson visits me, I investigate this drug case with her. We just found out that there might be this big drug ring that's run by a man named Anthony Hall. I got the first letter not long after we had figured out he was involved, and now I have this one, which says 'we wouldn't want anyone to get hurt, would we, Morgan Sadie Toner of Golden, Colorado'."

"That's exactly what it says?"

"Yes. I made my own decoder and checked it."

"And you didn't write it?"

"No."

"You're sure you're telling me the truth?" "Yes."

"You understand that you can get in trouble if you're not?"

"Yes, I understand."

"Okay, then. If you're sure, I can take this to get fingerprint tested." Jay took the note and walked out.

A few days later, Morgan was called into the office of the training center's behavioral specialist. The middle-aged blonde woman practically radiated irritation from behind her large mahogany desk.

"I swear I didn't write it."

"I don't know what to tell you," the woman said sharply. "The only fingerprints on the paper were yours, and you had access to black markers and a coder. I'm adding some time on to your stay here."

"Please, I promise I didn't write this. I'm scared someone's going to come try to kill me."

"Trust me, that's not going to happen here. I'm only going to add on an extra month, so be grateful I'm going easy on you."

Morgan's face felt hot as she was led out of the office. Restful nights were few and far between after that.

A few days later, Morgan sat in her room reading when a guard opened the door and tossed a paper at her without sparing a glance. Morgan's stomach dropped as she looked at the white envelope that had skidded across the floor. She got up from her bed to pick it up. Her first name was written in black marker on the front. She no longer had her makeshift decoder, nor the materials to make one, but she still slowly ripped it open. In the same handwriting all the others had been in, it said in plain English:

I told you to stop looking. From what I know, you have, for the most part. However, you'll soon be released. I have a feeling you'll give up the contents of this letter, and the other ones I sent you, so I'll say this: Stay out of my way, and maybe you won't see me soon.

Morgan let out the breath she was holding in. From what she briefly saw of the guard, she didn't recognize him. Maybe it was still possible to catch him before he left.

"Excuse me!" She hit the heel of her hand against the thick glass on the door. Eventually, Jay stopped in front of her door and opened it.

"What?" he asked flatly as he stopped in front of the room. Morgan waved the note at him.

"Someone in a guard uniform came by and gave this to me."

"How did you get that paper?"

"Like I said, someone just gave it to me."

"Another mafia note. Sure." He laughed humorlessly, plucking the paper from her hands. "And coincidentally not in code after you had your coloring book and cipher wheel taken away."

"Please, I know this sounds ridiculous, but I am not writing these!"

"I have a better guess. You really want some attention, and the positive kind wasn't good enough for you so you're still trying to milk some out of this drug ring story. Only your fingerprints were on that other paper. Now, I'm not going to tell my boss about this because frankly, I don't think you deserve the attention."

"Please just listen. Someone in a guard's uniform tossed it at me and walked away. I definitely didn't write it, so that means someone was either being very careless and let in someone that isn't supposed to be here, they were bribed, or maybe—"

"Whatever you say." Jay walked off down the hallway with the letter, scoffing.

...

Kipp hadn't realized it, but she had started to lean forward as Morgan was telling her story. She readjusted herself so that she wouldn't slide off the chair.

"Can you hold on for just a second? I'm going to make some calls so we can find out if those papers are still around." The detective paused the recording and walked a little way down the hall, leaving Kipp and Morgan alone.

"What is your scar from?" Kipp asked as the thought popped into her head. She hadn't really meant to say it out loud, but there was no taking it back now.

"I doubt that's part of the interview," Morgan said flatly. "But if you really want to know, the fault of this scar was that of an asshole with a pen. The asshole being my father."

Kipp opened her mouth to speak, but when nothing came out, she snapped it shut. *She sounds like some weird robot poet. And now I just have more questions.* Air from the vent above her blew against her neck like cold breath. The two sat in awkward silence for a few more seconds.

"Why?" was all Kipp could think to say. Morgan leaned back into her chair, sliding farther into the seat as she looked at Kipp.

"Let's just say my parents were not the best parents, or good people in general." Morgan's gaze seemed to travel behind Kipp's eyes as if searching for something. To Kipp's surprise, Morgan continued. "They wanted the 'perfect' daughter. One that would do all the chores in the house every day, act as a dress up doll that only wears frilly dresses, listen to every little thing her parents said even when it was destructive to her, and one that would get a rich husband in her early twenties so they could sit in a mansion during retirement. I was not that daughter, so they made me act like it. They're dead now though, so it doesn't really matter." Morgan averted her gaze as she uttered her last sentence and said no more. Kipp had more questions, but from Morgan's expression, she decided that it would be best to stay quiet.

The detective returned a minute later.

"All right, I'm back. They still have the notes!

We'll get them to the precinct before the end of the day. From the 'maybe you won't see me soon' it sounds like he's definitely planning on coming to Rundale at some point."

Kipp cleared her throat as she stood up. "Thanks for cooperating this time."

Morgan pursed her lips and looked away.

That night, Kipp found herself taking her questions to the packet Detective Caron had given her. She laid on her bed as she skimmed through the sparse contents of Morgan's psych evaluation by the warm light of the small chandelier.

Northeast Juvenile Center Psychiatric Exam

Name: Toner, Morgan S.

Date of birth: June 10th

Age: 13

Height/Weight: 5'0" / 78.4 lbs

Tests done: Clinical interview, IQ assessment

Test results: Psych evaluation: Not enough traits for diagnosis of any mental illness, but an anxious affect is present. IQ Evaluation: 124.

A few childhood pictures had been clipped to the records. Morgan didn't look genuinely happy in a single one. When Kipp looked closely at her school photos, she noticed that patches of foundation were dotted on Morgan's face.

The police file reported that Morgan's parents had been murdered in their house one night when she was eleven. She was twelve when she was arrested. Apparently, she was walking home from school one day because her foster mother was unable to pick her up. She was walking through an alleyway when a drunk man, Daniel Arlon, came up to her and pushed her against a wall. Morgan recalled to her lawyer that he touched her neck and grabbed her shoulders tight enough to leave marks. She fought back, kicking him in the groin when he put his hands on her waist. She ended up stabbing him in the neck with a piece of metal she found on the ground, causing him to eventually die from blood loss. Morgan was arrested later that day.

She refused to speak in the interrogation with police, and was given a lawyer. For months, she sat in a juvenile detention facility waiting to be brought before a judge. Although she was twelve, barely eligible to be tried as an adult, the district attorney decided against it. She accepted a plea deal, and was sentenced to five years in a juvenile training school for the murder of Arlon.

Kipp tossed the papers on her desk as she glanced at the time: 12:42 AM. She sat on her bed in silence. Milo eventually wandered up the stairs and into her room, wagging his tail. He jumped up on the bed and sat next to Kipp, laying his head in her lap. Kipp took his head in her hands, rubbing the sides of his face with her thumbs before getting up to turn off the light.

As she laid in bed, Kipp's head swirled with seemingly endless thoughts, and the visual of Morgan's icy eyes. She felt *bad.* It seemed like Morgan was never given a chance.

Finally, the release of sleep came, sending her to a desolate dreamland.

That night at the training school, Morgan was finishing some classes, taught to her by Detective Carson. Morgan had consistently felt unchallenged with the regular curriculum at the facility, and the detective had eventually stepped forward and offered to tutor her privately.

"I think we're almost ready to move onto the next unit," said Amelia, looking up from the sheet of problems she had given Morgan, all with check marks next to them.

"Detective?" Morgan asked, looking up from fiddling with her pencil.

"Yes?"

"What do you think I'll do when I'm released? Will I be able to go to college? How do I apply for that? Will a school even admit a criminal?"

"You'll be able to apply to have your record wiped," said Amelia, "but that could take a while. Fortunately, there's a number of schools that don't look at criminal records, especially from people's childhood, and a lot of people with criminal records get into schools that do look at those by making their applications about their crime and how they've changed."

Morgan's eyes widened. "Really?"

"Yes," the detective said with a soft smile, "and whatever school you decide to go to will be lucky to have you. I can help you with making a college list and doing applications if you want."

"Thank you, Detective."

An hour later, Morgan flipped the light off and climbed into bed, resting her hands on her stomach as she stared into the inky blackness of the ceiling and drifted off to sleep.

The peacefulness of her slumber was soon cut short by a dream.

She was standing in the kitchen of her parents' house and saw her father's blood-spattered face in front of her.

He kept saying the same thing. "I'm sorry, Morgan. I'm sorry. I'm sorry," he called, over and over again. Morgan broke away from her father's gaze, but she didn't see an exit she could run to like she had hoped. She looked to the side to see her old best friend, Serena. She tried to run to her but was frozen in place.

"What have you done, Morgan? What have you done?" Serena asked with a disgusted and horrified look before turning and walking away.

Morgan let out a silent scream for her to come back, straining for any sound to come out, but nothing more than a tiny squeak escaped. She looked back to her father and saw that he was now holding a knife. He took slow steps toward her, and Morgan once again tried to run, but it was as if she was trying to move through wet sand. She could only watch in horror as her father looked at her with a blank stare, raising the knife. Finally, her mind granted her mercy, and she woke with a jerk, a tear sliding its way down her cheek.

Her heart was pounding against her rib cage. She wrapped her arms around herself, gripping at her shoulders as she took deep breaths to slow her pulse. She wiped tears from her eyes, trying with minimal success to keep more from flowing. Morgan buried her face in her hands, keeping her sobs as close to silent as possible. She looked up from her hands once she could control her tears, and glanced at the alarm clock, casting an eerie red light on one side of the room. 4:38 AM. Lying back down, Morgan curled in on herself, letting one last tear fall down her face as she closed her eyes.

Chapter 5

Five years ago

Morgan was heading to the bus stop, eating a piece of cold toast as the wind nipped at her ears. Her shoes tapped on the concrete, and the morning air swirled around her exposed legs, causing goosebumps to prickle her skin. Her parents sent her to Jefferson County Day, a private school that was good for appearances. Instead of buses, they used cushy vans when parents couldn't drive their kid to school. The van that came to Morgan's area always stopped at the bus stop uphill from Morgan's house.

She could see it in the distance when she heard a familiar voice behind her.

"Toner! Jesus Christ, your skin is so pasty. I know you have, like, one friend, but you could stand to leave your house for other stuff once in a while."

By the time Morgan turned her head, she was already being shoved to the ground. The sidewalk scraped her knees, leaving blood on the pavement. Standing over her was Grace Monroe, who had tormented Morgan and her only friend, Serena, since they had started at Jefferson County Day in the sixth grade. Any time she spent at school was hell with Grace around. There were endless insults, hair pulling, and even hits from Grace and her friends if Serena or Morgan tried to fight back. No one else wanted to stick up for them. Morgan was enough of a target already with her obnoxious dresses and quiet nature, but her propensity for tears only made it worse.

Grace's shoe connected with the side of Morgan's face, sending pain across her cheekbone. Morgan groaned and put a hand over her face. She tried to stand up only to be pinned down by Grace stomping her foot down on her lower back, causing a dull pain to spread through it. Grace's dirty-blonde hair swished to the side as she yanked Morgan's ponytail up and pulled out a pair of scissors. She cut crudely through the hair right above the elastic band, letting chunks falling onto Morgan's back and the surrounding sidewalk.

Morgan's knees stung as the already broken skin was pressed into the sidewalk. She gave up fighting. There was no way to undo the damage now.

When Grace was done, she pocketed the scissors, letting out what Morgan could only describe as a cackle as she walked over Morgan to the bus stop.

Morgan pushed herself off the ground. She wiped blood from her legs with the inside of her dress, inhaling through her teeth.

"Morgan? What happened?"

Morgan looked up to see Serena hurrying down the sidewalk from the bus stop. "What did you do?" Serena said loudly to Grace, who promptly kicked her in the shins, effectively tripping her on the inclined sidewalk, and continued walking. Serena got up, ignoring the newly made scuffs on the palms of her hands. "Asshole," she hissed. She continued towards Morgan, shoving locks of frizzy brown hair out of her face.

"Hi," Morgan said, voice cracking.

"What happened?" Serena asked. Morgan brushed at her choppy hair with one hand, realizing the degree to which it was ruined. She could already feel her mother's wooden spoon connecting with her ribs.

"My mother is going to lose her mind when she sees this, and even worse, she's probably going to blame it on me."

Serena balled her fists up, pursing her lips. "I know I keep saying this, but you need to tell someone about how your parents treat you. What if one day they accidentally go too far? I'm honestly really close to telling someone myself."
"No! You can't! If you do that and they find out, it isn't going to be worth it. I won't be friends with you

anymore if you do that."

"Okay, fine, I won't. But you need to stand up for yourself. And about Grace, at this point we really should just go to the principal or something."

"Grace's parents give a lot of money to the school. I've tried to tell the principal, but as long as she isn't trying to kill us, he won't do anything to risk the funds they're getting."

"I should get you some ice for that," she said finally, pointing to Morgan's quickly bruising eye. "If you want, we can go to my house. My parents aren't home, so you don't have to worry about them telling your parents."

"That would be nice," Morgan replied. They began walking up the street to Serena's house, over the smears of blood left on the sidewalk. They passed the bus stop, and looked on as the van's figure shrank further into the shine of the morning sun.

"I guess we'll have to walk to school today," said Morgan.

"Yeah… Or we could skip a day. It's the first day, it's not like there's going to be tests or assignments." She unlocked the door to her house and they both went inside.

"Why are there so many boxes?" Morgan said, looking around at where the furniture used to be.

"I… should've found a way to tell you this sooner," Serena began. "I'm moving. At the end of last year, I told my parents about Grace and they freaked out.

I thought they were going to talk to the principal, but a few weeks ago they said they're going to try to put me in a new school before this school year. It's in Grand Junction. I told them I didn't want to leave, but they didn't listen. I promise I'll visit as much as I can. We can send letters to each other if you want. I can also give you my phone number so you can call me."

"Okay," Morgan said quietly. That was the only thing she could get out as she stared at the boxes.

"Are you okay? I really don't want you to be alone."

"I'll be fine. Did you say you had ice?"

Serena gave Morgan a washcloth filled with ice cubes and the two sat down across from each other on the floor.

"I have an idea, what if I call the school and imitate your mom and say you're sick?" said Serena.

"I guess that has a chance of working, but what if I miss something important in class?"

"Come on, you have to live a little. You're one of the best students in the school. I'm sure you'll be fine."

"I hope. My parents won't like it if my grades drop below an A. They never stop badgering me about finishing my homework and studying because it would be 'embarrassing' for them if I didn't do well in school."

"Wow. They even make your academic success about them," said Serena. "I'm seriously worried about what might happen after I move. I at least want to be able to leave knowing you're okay. We can call the police right now and get your parents locked up!"

"And what if what my parents do isn't considered child abuse and people just view it as harsh discipline?"

"They scream at you when you don't do something exactly the way they like it, and they beat you when you mildly disobey! That *has* to be considered child abuse."

"Yes, but, even if they did lose custody of me, where would I go? Child services would probably send me to live with my aunt and uncle or something, and nothing would be any different. They're just like my parents."

"If you tell them that, they might put you in foster care, then you'd be with a family that actually takes care of you. If I tell my parents, then we could probably work together to get some evidence against your parents, and maybe—"

"Please just stop!" Morgan yelled. There was no way scheming like that could end well. Living with her relatives would be awful, and if she was by some miracle put into the foster system, it was a lottery whether or not she'd be put with a loving family.

Serena sighed in defeat, but said nothing, looking to the ground. Morgan held back tears. She never wanted to yell, especially at her only friend, but she had to get Serena to stop somehow.

Morgan removed the washcloth from her face, revealing a magenta bruise right on her cheekbone. She set the wet cloth on the table.

"We should probably call the school to say why you aren't going to be there today," said Serena.

She made the call with a surprisingly good imitation of Morgan's mother.

"What do you want to do now?" Morgan asked.

Serena rested her chin on her hand for a second. "I can probably fix your hair. I could even it out. I've practiced on myself before," she said, perking up.

"It might lessen the blow for my parents if it's not all crooked," Morgan said in contemplation. "Let's try it."

Serena pulled a chair into her bathroom for Morgan to sit on while she cut her hair.

"You can sit down, and I'll go grab a spray bottle to wet your hair so it'll make it a little easier to cut," said Serena. Morgan sat in the chair, drumming her fingers on her leg as she waited for Serena to come back. Her hair looked *awful*. It was longer on one side, with countless locks being much longer or shorter than the surrounding ones. "Got it!" Serena popped back into the room, a newly filled spray bottle in hand. She wrapped a towel around Morgan's shoulders to keep the water from dripping on her clothes.

When Serena was finished, Morgan's hair hung just below her ears. It was choppy, but not too bad.

"It looks so much better! Thank you," Morgan exclaimed. "This is going to be so much easier to deal with than when my hair was long."

Serena smiled. "I'm glad I could help," she replied. "Hey, do you want to get some frozen yogurt? I have some money saved that we can use."

"Okay!"

Morgan and Serena walked to the nearby frozen yogurt shop. They made their bowls, Morgan getting a plain bowl of pomegranate, and Serena seemingly trying to fit every flavor and topping into her cup.

After Serena paid for their yogurt, they both sat down in the tall plastic chairs at one of the tables, neither of them speaking.

"I don't want you to worry about me," Morgan said into the silence.

"I can't really help it. You need to talk to someone other than me," Serena countered.

"Please, can we drop this now?" Morgan's voice was almost too calm for this sort of conversation. Serena didn't say anything more on the matter. Her phone buzzed on the table. She picked it up and grimaced.

"What is it?" asked Morgan.

"Grace. She keeps messaging me. I've tried to block the account, but the same person keeps writing from different ones. She used to text me, but I guess she ran out of numbers to text me from or something because I blocked a bunch and she stopped. She's doing it from Instagram now. She said, 'Hey, why didn't you come to school today? What did you think of Morgan's hair? I think I did a great job lmfao.' I'll block this one too. Maybe she'll get bored of making hundreds of spam accounts soon."

"Maybe," said Morgan.

Serena glanced at the time. "It's only ten thirty. What do you want to do?"

Morgan shrugged. "Do you have a chess set at your house?"

"Yeah! Let's go back and we can play!"

After getting back to Serena's house, Serena rushed into another room and came back with a wooden chess set and put it down on the floor. The two set up the pieces and began to play.

"How do you *always* win?" Serena asked with folded arms as Morgan checkmated her.

"Strategic thinking and a little creativity," Morgan answered simply. "Want to play again?"

"You're on."

They continued to play for nearly three hours, taking breaks to watch some TV. Serena looked especially happy seeing Morgan laugh without hesitation. It was the most fun Morgan had in years. She was even able to get an apple from the fridge without worry.

"Do you want to get lunch?" Morgan asked.

"I think we have some leftovers if you're okay with pizza."

"It will probably be better than the cafeteria food," Morgan said with a smile.

The food was indeed much better than what was served at the school cafeteria. Morgan and Serena watched TV for a while after they ate, mostly laughing at the absurd reality shows that were on.

Morgan tried not to think about the fact that this might be the last time they could spend time together like this. What was she going to do without Serena? She felt like she'd go insane without a single person to actually talk to. Maybe she could stick it out until she could make some new friends in high school.

"I should probably get home." Morgan stood up.

"Wait, I have to give you my phone number." Serena tore off a piece of paper towel and wrote out her number in Sharpie. They looked at each other and paused for a second before stepping closer into a tight hug.

"I had a great time," Morgan said, folding up the paper towel to put in her pocket.

"That's good," said Serena, opening the door for her. As Morgan walked away, she turned around for a second to see Serena's bittersweet smile shrink into an empty shade of sadness.

Tears rolled down Morgan's cheeks, leaving streaks in their wake as she sat on the end of her bed. She had gone to school the next day, and foolishly hoped the whole time that Serena would show up, but she never did. The paper towel had been folded up and hidden inside a yellow mechanical pencil from the bottom of her backpack.

"Morgan, put on this dress right now! You're going to make us late," said her mother. Morgan slowly looked up from the newspaper, her eyes red and swollen. She only stared at the dress. It was an unfavorable shade of green with scratchy lace on the neck and sleeves.

"Now!" her mother yelled. "And wipe those tears off. Your eyes better be dried up by the time we get in the car or I'll really give you something to cry about." Morgan's mother thrust the dress at her. "Put it on. Stop acting like a toddler, you're eleven years old for God's sake."

"Morgan! Do what your mother says!" her father yelled, landing a hard smack to Morgan's face, snapping her head to the side. Morgan quickly took the dress from her mother, holding one hand to her stinging cheek.

Stomach twisting in disgust at the piece of clothing she was wearing, Morgan exited her room.

"Aww, you look so cute!" Her mother smiled, handing Morgan her shoes to put on. Morgan took the Mary Janes, shoes that had rubbed her heels raw more times than she could count, many times not letting the wound heal before being worn again.

Morgan got in the back seat of her parents' car, the backs of her shoes already scraping ruthlessly against her skin.

At the restaurant, Morgan's parents ordered steaks, but as Morgan began to order, she was interrupted by her mother,

"And she'll have a Caesar salad."

Morgan suppressed a glare as shc took her utensils out of the napkin roll. Once in a great while, she would succeed at putting in an order for herself, but no matter what food she, or her parents ordered for her, they would only allow her to eat a certain portion of it. If Morgan ate more than that, she would be yanked out of the restaurant, and face serious consequences at home.

Their waiter soon arrived with their food. Morgan was able to eat half of it before her parents stopped her. She became more and more aware of the smells from others' plates as she stared at her own, hand itching to grab the fork again. With every move she made, she saw her parents' eyes glance over, waiting like a viper to snatch a utensil out of her hand. Hunger was still gnawing at her stomach, making her head feel fuzzy as if it was stuffed with cotton.

The family eventually drove home, but not before Morgan's parents ordered dessert for themselves.

Morgan retreated to her room as soon as they got back. She marched in and pulled out some clothes from a bin she'd hidden deep in her closet, filled with only four items that Serena bought for her at a thrift store: jeans, a black T-shirt, some too-big sneakers and a black hoodie. Maybe she'd be able to wear them for her first day back at school tomorrow, being that she skipped the official first day. She could hide the clothes in her backpack and put them on when she got to school. That thought immediately met a tragic end as her mother swung her door open.

"Morgan, you—" Her face contorted into a sneer as her eyes caught the clothes. "What are those? You are absolutely not wearing *that*. Where did they even come from? Because I definitely didn't buy them for you." She snatched the clothes from Morgan's arms, tossing them to the floor. "I'm throwing those away. Lay this out for tomorrow." Her mother pulled out a frilly, pink dress, one that would certainly attract some torments from Grace.

"Mother, may I please wear something more casual?" Morgan asked with a sudden bout of confidence.

"Morgan, don't argue with me," her mother warned. Just then, Morgan's father stepped into the room.

"What the hell is she doing?" he said. "She had a pair of ratty jeans and some baggy old sweatshirt hidden in her closet," her mother said, crossing her arms.

"Are you trying to look like a heathen? A druggie or something? You are not wearing that shit to school!" he shouted.

"I—" Morgan started to argue, but her father's slap cut her off. "Fath—" Morgan tried again. This time, a fist connected with her face, and Morgan could feel her lip sting as it was split. With Serena's words in her head, Morgan snapped. "I *wish* you were drunks! Then CPS would take me away so I wouldn't have to wait until I was eighteen to get away from you! You're crazy! You—" She stopped herself as fear panged in her chest. Her father, now red-faced with fury, reeled his arm back.

The blow sent her to the floor, where a foot met with her stomach, and then with her nose. She regretted even pulling out the bin. Pain exploded across her entire body as blows hit her all around. Her pleas for mercy did nothing as she curled tightly into a ball with hands covering her head. She tried to pretend she was at Serena's house, laughing at cheesy commercials.

A particularly hard kick to her spine knocked the air from her lungs, taking away her ability to even cry out in pain. She gulped down air when her lungs would allow it and eventually found her voice again.

"I'm sorry! I'm sorry! I'll wear it! I'm sorry, I'm sorry, I'm sorry, I'm *sorry*. I'll wear the dress… Please stop… *Please*," Morgan choked out.

Finally, the blows stopped coming.

"Damn right you will, and you won't be getting breakfast or dinner tomorrow, so you better eat a good fucking lunch at school! Don't ever fucking talk to us like that again!" Her father gave her one last kick to the stomach before walking out. She looked up to see her mother give a disapproving shake of her head before slamming the door behind her.

Morgan stayed lying on the floor for a while, wheezing in breaths while her face remained pressed against the scratchy carpet. She sobbed, licking the metallic-tasting liquid from her lips and brushing the fresh blood falling from her nose. It had never been this bad before.

A second passed, and Morgan stared at her backpack, wondering how much it would hurt if she drove a sharpened pencil down the veins in her arm and waited for death. *No. God, no I can't. I don't want to die.*

A thought wormed its way into her mind. *If* they *died, then I wouldn't have to deal with them anymore.* She shook her head in some attempt to remove the idea from her mind. *No, I can't* kill *them. Can I?*

No. *Stop. I* can't.

Well, Serena is gone, I don't have anyone else in my life that will take care of me.

No.

But, if I kill them, at least when I get caught, and go to prison I won't be hit every day, and I'll actually get fed decent portions of food.

No, *no, Mother and Father are just misled. They're still people.*

They're... bad *people.*

Morgan clenched her teeth. *What if one day they snap and just kill me? This might be the only opportunity I have to get away.*

Chapter 6

Present day

The light scraping sounds of pencils on paper were the only thing that could be heard in the room as Kipp's calculus class continued through their quiz. Once she finished, she was told to sit quietly for the remainder of class.

Eyes drifting to the window, Kipp stared at the bushes that grew on the other side of the glass. She watched as birds flew by and leaves bristled in the wind, but most of all, she thought of Morgan. She couldn't tell what Morgan thought of her, and it was driving her insane. Morgan didn't really seem to like her, yet she'd tolerated her enough to answer her question, and a personal one at that. Kipp didn't understand it. There was a part of her that wanted to get to know Morgan, that wanted to see her again. Was that bad?

When class let out, Kipp met up with Nikki, Luke

and Isabel in the hallway to head to lunch.

"How do you think you did?"

"I better have done good," Nikki answered. "My mom made me study for that for like, three hours last night."

"Hey, I think they have those garlic rolls today!" Isabel exclaimed, pointing to the end of the line for food.

"Yes! Those are always so good," said Kipp. At that moment, a group of freshmen walked by, talking and laughing as they carried their plates to a nearby table.

"Kipp! You see that freshman in the white shirt?" Nikki asked. Kipp looked to where she was subtly gesturing and nodded.

"Yeah?" Kipp confirmed.

"Doesn't she look like Hannah from middle school?"

"I guess," Kipp said flatly.

"Reminds me of the good ole' days. You remember that sleepover we had?"

"Yep."

"Who's Hannah?" asked Luke.

"She was this girl that was in me and Kipp's middle school friend group who was kind of a bitch, to put it bluntly," said Nikki.

"What happened with her?" Isabel asked as they started walking to a table.

"It wasn't even just her," said Nikki. "I mean, it

was mainly her, but everyone else either supported her or didn't really say anything when she was mean."

"What kinds of things would she say?" Luke asked.

"There was one time when Kipp told everyone how she made the basketball team and then Hannah was like, 'You're gonna be too muscle-y, and boys don't like that.'"

"Ew," Luke responded, brushing light brown curls out of his eyes.

Any thoughts of Hannah instantly made Kipp irritated. Especially after Hannah's remark and the rest of the group's defense of her, it was clear that the group was filled with people that Kipp and Nikki did not want to be around. It wasn't hard to put distance between them, considering the rest of the group began to exclude them from out-of-school activities. They soon cut ties altogether.

Kipp barely thought about Hannah anymore, but there was a time when she would have considered her one of her closest friends. It was interesting how fast one could lose a friend group after just one incident.

Kipp had finished most of her homework before lacrosse that day, and now at home, was finding herself bored enough to do one of the bonus questions that came with her calculus worksheet. On impulse, she sat up and walked to the front door, leaving her work sitting on the kitchen table. *Where to go, where to go.* She began tapping her foot on the porch as she looked around.

Morgan. Kipp paused. Why was that her first thought? *It couldn't do any harm.* After all, she did want to talk to her to ask a few more questions. *Hopefully she'll answer them, even if they're personal.* Kipp went back inside to grab her helmet, jumped on her bike and started riding toward the NJC. She pedaled faster than normal, fueled by the strange giddiness that had set in, even as she expected to be turned away.

Kipp was told she'd be able to request to speak with Morgan, but that Morgan could refuse or end the meeting at any time.

Kipp was guided to a meeting room and asked to stay there while the workers went to fetch Morgan. Kipp was left alone to wait. She looked around the small room, shifting around on the polished wooden bench and tapping her fingers on the table made of the same material.

The door opened, and Detective Carson stepped through, shutting it behind her.

"Hi Kipp, I heard you came in wanting to talk with Morgan?"

"Oh, hey. Yeah, I was just curious about a few things."

"I wanted to talk to you about something. About Morgan, that is."

"Sure. What's up?"

"I noticed you were a little short with her," the detective said, speaking slowly. "I know that you were probably a little ramped up, ready to interrogate people who are going to be all defiant and snarky, but Morgan isn't like that. She had a very rough childhood, and though she *is* a convicted killer which isn't easily excusable… it's not like she killed that man for no reason. She was only twelve when it happened and she was really scared. What I'm trying to say is that deep down, she's a good person. She's afraid of being hurt again. I don't want her to be treated like a monster." The detective's eyes locked onto Kipp's. Kipp shrunk back a fraction. She had been a little nicer the second time she talked to Morgan, but her first meeting probably wasn't the best first impression. She didn't *want* Morgan to hate her, although she wouldn't care if she did. At least, that's what she told herself.

"I'll be more patient," Kipp said.

"Good." The detective stood up. "Because if I hear that you berated her, I will make sure she doesn't have to interact with you again."

Kipp smiled nervously. "I definitely won't."

Amelia flashed her a thin smile and closed the door.

A few minutes later, the door was opened by a worker, who allowed Morgan to walk into the room before closing it, leaving her and Kipp by themselves.

Kipp sat up straight in her chair with her hands folded on the table.

"What do you want?" Morgan asked almost accusingly when she sat down. She crossed her arms, but didn't wrap them around herself.

"I wanted to ask you about your life."

The bored look on Morgan's was replaced by one of confusion.

"Why?" she asked.

"I had some questions about you. I read a little about you from some stuff Detective Carson gave me, and I thought your life was really interesting, and I wanted to ask you some questions about it," Kipp said with a hopeful look. Morgan sighed, but her expression softened.

"Back with the personal questions again," she said, and Kipp could almost see a smile tugging at the corners of her lips. "Go ahead and ask them."

"Huh. I was ninety-nine percent sure you were going to say no."

"Well, you asked nicely, and you're not being unnecessarily harsh. Detective Carson brought to my attention that you were probably prepared to talk to an extremely unpleasant person. Not that I can't be extremely unpleasant at times, but you know what I mean."

"Yeah," Kipp responded. "So, the first question…" She pulled a sheet of crumpled paper out of her pocket containing the questions she had compiled.

"What's your favorite color?"

"My favorite color?" Morgan squinted.

"Not all the questions are going to be super personal." Kipp laughed softly.

"It's navy blue." Morgan's face became something a little closer to a smile, with her brows lifting further away from her eyes, and her lips perking up at the corners. Kipp scribbled down her answer.

"What's your favorite color?" Morgan asked when Kipp looked up from her notepad.

"Orange," Kipp answered with a smile. "If you could travel anywhere in the world, where would you go?" she continued.

"I don't know… Maybe somewhere in New York?"

"Upstate or city?"

"Either one, honestly. Although I have heard the Catskills are nice," Morgan answered.

"Yeah, they are," Kipp agreed.

"You've been?"

"No, but I've seen pictures," Kipp stated matter-of-factly, a humorous undertone in her voice. "Have you been able to go anywhere since you were arrested?"

"No, not really." Morgan's almost-smile disappeared.

"Well, I hope you get to do some traveling when you get out. Uh, last time I was here, you talked about how your parents were super controlling and stuff.

Could you… say more?" Kipp hesitated, becoming concerned that her question was too blunt.

"They used their fists as a convincing factor for me to fit their model of a perfect child and didn't let me eat a healthy amount of food. That's really all there is to it."

"That sounds awful." Kipp's brows knitted together as she imagined the life Morgan had lived.

"At least they can't hurt me anymore, can they?" Morgan said dryly, breaking eye contact.

Kipp couldn't think of anything to say.

"You know," Morgan continued, "I can't look at the color pink without cringing. It's just a stupid color, and I can't even *look* at it." Morgan discreetly wrapped her arms around herself as if searching for comfort. "Sorry, I'm getting off topic. Do you have any more questions?" Her eyes looked as if all the joy had been drained out of them as she. Kipp was silent for a while before blurting out her final question.

"One more. Why did you kill that person?"

"Why?" Morgan echoed.

"Yeah."

Morgan's gaze immediately fell to the floor. "I was blinded with fear, I suppose. I don't think I really thought about what the consequences would be if I accidentally went that far. I wish I only used enough force to protect myself, and let that man get arrested." She shifted in her seat, letting out a slow exhalation. "The thing is, people always tell stories to kids about monsters that live under their beds and in their closets, then the kids get older, and they begin to believe that monsters aren't real, only to quickly find that monsters are real. *Real* monsters are people that do so much harm without giving a damn. I didn't want to feel the pain of it all anymore. I thought getting rid of the people that hurt me would fix it, or help make it better. But it didn't. It made everything so much worse."

Kipp could see tears forming in Morgan's eyes as her voice cracked when she finished her sentence. *People.* Kipp's eyes narrowed a fraction as her thoughts hung onto that word. Morgan turned to the side on the bench she sat on, her hair falling in front of her face, only partly hiding the tears spilling over.

"It's… I didn't— I—" She desperately tried wiping the tears on her face, straining to keep more from flowing. Kipp didn't know what possessed her to do it, but she got up, and circled around the table, sliding onto Morgan's bench. Morgan looked up in bewilderment, trying to even out her breathing. Kipp slowly pulled Morgan into a hug, giving her time to pull away if she so desired.

Morgan froze, and for a moment, the only thing that could be heard in the room was her ragged breathing. Her eyes were wide, and her mouth was slightly parted, but she eventually squeezed them both shut as she melted into the embrace. She tucked her arms into her chest, a quiet whimper escaping.

Kipp's hand moved to rest on the back of Morgan's head like one would with an infant, her other arm staying curled around the girl's back. Kipp felt tears of her own creep forward with every whimper and sob that came from the girl she held to her chest. Thankfully, Morgan sniffled, and pulled away before any tears could spill over from Kipp's eyes. Morgan looked at Kipp for a second, as if in contemplation.

"Sorry," she mumbled, glancing away.

"All good," said Kipp. A beat passed as Kipp struggled to think of what she should do next. She settled on standing up and bringing over a box of tissues from a nearby windowsill. Morgan wiped her eyes with her sleeve and blew her nose. Once Kipp could see that her eyes were fully dry, she ripped a piece off her legal pad and scribbled on it before sliding it over to Morgan.

"I've got to go, my mom doesn't know I'm here, but there's my number if you want to talk sometime."

Morgan looked over at the paper and then back up at Kipp, who looked down at her with a smile. Kipp paused before she exited, looking back over her shoulder to see Morgan wave goodbye, a barely noticeable, but still present smile on her face.

It's kind of understandable if she did kill them, Kipp thought on the way back.

No. Nope. Stop. Don't side with her.

But they did kind of *deserve it.*

Kipp tore her thoughts away. Her stomach continued to flip, thinking about Morgan's indirect confession, but she couldn't ignore the way her heart had swelled when Morgan accepted the comfort she'd offered her, and the way her stomach *fluttered* when Morgan smiled at her. It was strange to say the least.

Kipp met her friends for a movie night at Nikki's house later that day. At Nikki's suggestion, they were planning on having an old horror movie marathon, but Kipp found herself unable to fully focus on the bloody and occasionally badly acted scenes in front of her. A small voice in the back of her head asked if the way Morgan murdered her parents was at all similar. She tapped her fingers on her cheek as her attention finally started to take hold. Suddenly, everyone in the room flinched at a jumpscare, Kipp almost poking herself in the eye.

When the movies were over, Nikki drove Kipp back to her house.

"Has anything happened with that case?" Nikki asked as they pulled out of the driveway.

"The girl down at the juvie center, Morgan Toner, the one I talked about at breakfast the other day, agreed to another interview." Kipp talked fast, eager to overshadow her original description of Morgan. "She said that the notes she got said Hall was coming to Rundale and thinks they're coming after her. She talked about how she got involved in this because she helped the police with their drug ring investigation."

"They have a murderer doing detective work?" Nikki joked.

"She's being helpful. She's smart, too. She helped the department find out Hall was involved in the first place," Kipp said.

Nikki's eyes squinted a fraction, as if she was expecting Kipp to laugh along.

"Even if she's smart, how do you know she won't lie about stuff?" said Nikki.

"She's not that kind of person. She wants to help."

"Yeah but how do you know?" Nikki prodded, a bit of the humor leaving her voice.

"I just do!" Kipp said sharply.

"Okay, damn." Nikki shook her head.

The two didn't exchange words when Kipp exited the car at her house.

Morgan ate dinner slowly on her lonely end of the table. The dining hall had four long, plastic tables. Morgan always sat at the one closest to the dorms. She never met anyone she wanted to sit by, but she couldn't help but feel envious of the people able to laugh and talk while they ate. At least she could say she's had one positive interaction with someone her age. Kipp had surprised her. That was the first time

Morgan had been hugged in years. As she continued eating, the fragments that had come to her mind when she was crying fully formed into memories.

The more she had looked at the knife, the more her smile grew. *They're not going to be able to hurt me anymore. No more.* She walked quietly to her parents' bedroom, holding her breath as she turned the knob.

The room was dark, with only the red glow of the alarm clock to light up the room before Morgan let in the light from the kitchen. Morgan's mother was closest to the door. She was sleeping on her side, so Morgan had to angle the knife to get it right at the dip in her throat. With a deep breath, Morgan jerked the knife back and drove it into her mother's throat. Her eyes flew open as she started struggling to breathe through the blood gathering in her airway. Morgan ran to the other side of the bed, figuring the wet gasps from her mother would be enough to wake her father up. She felt sick hearing the sounds. When she got there, in the small amount of light provided by the open bedroom door, she saw that her father's eyes were open.

Morgan's breathing was turning into quiet mewls, but she shakily raised the knife, hoping she'd be quick enough to just get it over with. She managed to stab him once in the side of the neck before she pulled back when he tried to grab her wrist. He ran his hand across the nightstand and gripped an expensive fountain pen. He ripped off the cap right as Morgan jumped on the bed and lunged at him again. Her father drove the pen into her cheekbone and dragged it down her face. She felt like her chest was caving in as her heart seemed to heat up from beating so fast.

Inky blood began to trickle down, soaking into Morgan's shirt. Morgan screamed, slashing his hand. Her father grabbed her wrist, stabbing at it with the pen. The pain barely registered to Morgan at that point. She just wanted it to be over. Why couldn't he just *die?* Morgan switched the knife to her other hand and reeled it back, pretending to go for her father's stomach, but pulled it back at the last second and plunged it into her father's throat. The pen fell from his hand onto the bedspread. Morgan grabbed it as he fruitlessly struggled to stop the blood pouring from his neck.

As she watched her father slowly going limp, Morgan stood up, trembling. She slid off the bed, clutching the knife and pen so hard that her fingers hurt. Her clothes were spattered with her father's blood, and her face was covered with her own. She staggered into the bathroom, and dropped the knife and pen into the sink as she looked at herself in the mirror. There was a deep gash on her face which she hastily covered up with some medical tape from under the sink, also wrapping part of her arm where it was hit by the pen.

Morgan examined her violently shaking, bloody hands through the tears now blurring her vision.

She couldn't control her breathing anymore, and it morphed into shallow gasps that only got faster and faster. *What do I do now? I can't just sit here. If I get arrested, I'll get decent food and I won't end up with bruises because I didn't listen to my parents, but that's not a guarantee that I won't get abused. If they try me as an adult I could be in there for a really long time.* Morgan's thoughts were cut off as she picked up the knife and pen and walked slowly back into the bedroom. She only stood in the doorway, not wanting to make eye contact with her mother's corpse, which was now lying splayed on the floor.

She heard a raspy breath and turned to see her father looking at her.

"Please call an ambulance. I'm sorry, Morgan. I'm sorry. I'm sorry." Her father shuddered, words distorted from the blood still dripping from his mouth. Morgan stiffened as hot tears mixed with the blood and ink on her face.

"No you're not," she whispered.

Chapter 7

Tick. Tick. Tick. Tick. It was a boring noise, but for Morgan, it was a reminder of time crawling closer to when she would be released. She brushed her teeth and ran a comb through her hair in front of the communal bathroom mirror for the last time. After putting both items in a small bag, she was officially packed up to go. What kind of foster family would they put her with? Would they be like the last one she had? Morgan didn't allow herself to expect anything better. That would only mean more disappointment if they weren't. She looked around the dorm as she waited, taking in the empty walls and plain floor. A guard opened the door and Morgan got off the bed.

"Here's your personal belongings," he said, thrusting a plastic bag at her. It was the only thing Morgan had on her when she was arrested: her old backpack. "Your foster mother is waiting outside. I hope I don't see you back here. Good luck," said the guard. They walked into the lobby where Amelia

Carson was standing.

"Surprise!" Amelia waved as Morgan walked over to her, mouth parted.

"Are you fostering me?" she asked.

"Yes. I registered as a foster parent a while ago so I could take you when you got out. I thought you'd probably prefer me over a random foster family. But if not, then—"

"No! No, it's great. I would definitely prefer to stay with you."

As they stood up to leave, Morgan let out a small laugh out of sheer shock.

"Well? How does it feel to be out?" asked Amelia.

"Good," Morgan replied, feeling her smile grow.

"Want to go to my house so you can drop your stuff off?"

"Sure, but are you positive I wouldn't be a burden living with you? I don't want to cause you extra stress or anything."

"Well, I'm expecting to get a promotion soon, that is, if I've passed the sergeant's exam. And even if I don't, I'll still be able to support both of us. I made this decision a while ago. Trust me, you aren't going to be a burden."

"But what about Hall? I still don't know how he got the notes to me, or how he knew I was involved in the first place. What if he tracks me down and finds your house?"

"I won't let that happen. I will do everything in

my power to make sure both of us are safe."

Morgan's imagination was already starting to run wild with thoughts about what her new life would be like: being able to eat and sleep when she wanted, the ability to walk around outside, no more learning trades. It sounded like heaven.

"Thank you so much, Detective."

"You can call me Amelia, you know," she said with a laugh.

The detective held the door of her house open for Morgan as she stepped through. The house had a mostly tan color scheme, with some pops of color: blue throw pillows on the couch and a few decorative vases standing on a shelf.

"I have an extra bedroom down the hall there. I've been using it as a guest room, but now you can have it."

"Really?" Morgan whispered absentmindedly, looking from the hall back to Amelia.

"Of course. If I have any friends over that need to stay the night, they can sleep on the couch. You can go ahead and put your stuff down in there. The sheets are clean. Come on." She gestured for Morgan to follow her, turning lights on in the dim hall as she went. "Here's the bathroom," she said, pointing to a slightly ajar door to Morgan's right, "and *here* is your room." She opened another door right next to the bathroom to reveal a tidy room with a queen bed in the center, its black headboard flush with the wall. The cover had a black and white pattern, and two large decorative pillows that matched its mandala design. The carpet was white, and looked very soft. The only thing that gave her pause was the pink floral quilt folded across the end of the bed. She hadn't realized that her eyes were stuck on it until Amelia said something.

"Is there something wrong?" Amelia asked.

"No, no. It's nothing," Morgan replied.

"If you have a question, or there's something you don't like, we can fix it."

"Can… Can I take the pink quilt off the bed? Like, out of the room?" Morgan asked timidly.

"Absolutely." Amelia immediately pulled the quilt off, tossing it over her shoulder. "This thing doesn't go with the color scheme anyway."

"Thank you," said Morgan. The breath she had been holding in spilled out. Her parents wouldn't have *had* different covers to use, let alone let her change them.

Amelia couldn't help but smile as Morgan set her bag down and began excitedly looking around the room, running her hand over the curtains, the closet door, and the bed, only stopping at the TV to avoid getting it smudged. Morgan found her mind drifting to the memory of her old room, with its pink and green bed sheets and closet stuffed full of itchy dresses.

"This is great," she murmured.

"I want you to know that this is your house too now. You have access to all the food and drinks, you can watch TV whenever you want. The only rules I'll have for you are don't use the stove when I'm not here, and remember to keep the doors and windows locked. I'm pretty sure you know all the obvious stuff, like don't walk all around the house with muddy shoes and don't just leave spilled stuff on the floor."

"Of course. Do you know if I'll be going to a real school?"

"You're legally allowed to not go to school at this age, but I have a feeling you won't want to do that. We could put you in the school we're in the district for, or you could stay home and do online homeschool."

"I think I'd prefer to stay home."

"Okay, but I do want to warn you, it'll be difficult to get into college with your criminal record not being expunged or sealed."

Morgan wanted to be optimistic, but what Amelia said worried her. Still, she responded with: "If all else fails, I can go to community college or online school."

"Well, then, we can set you up in an online school by next week."

"How long will you be gone during the day?" Morgan wondered what it would be like being completely alone for the first time in over five years. It sounded nice.

"I usually work from nine to five."

"Could I come with you on some days?"

"Yeah, you can bring your school stuff and work on it in the precinct. You can come with me every day if you're nervous about being home alone. I want you to be comfortable living here, so I want you to let me know if there's anything I can do to make this transition better."

Morgan smiled. "I can't think of anything else you would be able to do. Everything you've already done is amazing. Should I put my stuff away?"

"Yeah. And let me know if you need anything like lotion or mouthwash. There's bottles of body wash and shampoo and conditioner already in there."

Morgan set the bag with her toothbrush and comb on the bathroom counter. She took a moment to look at her old backpack, still contained in the plastic bag. It probably still had dried blood on it somewhere. She decided to slide it under the bed.

"Do you want me to show you the rest of the house," Amelia asked.

Morgan walked through various rooms with Amelia: the living room, kitchen, the master bedroom, and the garage. Finally, Amelia led Morgan back to her room.

"If you need me, I'll be in the living room." Amelia smiled. Morgan nodded, walking over to the bed.

She climbed onto the covers and laid down, looking up to the ceiling. She folded her hands over her stomach, took a deep breath, and closed her eyes.

Morgan was woken up by Amelia's voice from down the hall.

"Morgan? I've made some food if you'd like any."

Morgan sat up. The room had gotten dark. Outside, there was a dull orange glow of the set sun, but it did little to illuminate the room. Morgan walked toward the shine of the light coming from out in the hallway.

"There you are. Come on over." Amelia gestured to a chair at the small kitchen table. Morgan sat, and Amelia placed a bowl of spaghetti in front of her.

"Thank you so much," Morgan said, lifting her fork to begin eating.

It was one of the best feelings she had ever experienced. Sitting at an actual kitchen table, the sensation of warm food filling her stomach, knowing she could savor each bite was wonderful. "Has there been any movement with the Hall case?"

"Not much." Amelia sighed. "We've moved away from trying to find storage areas for the drugs and focusing more on finding dealers so we can hopefully get some more information on the inner workings of the operation. You should come by the precinct with me sometime. Maybe you can help us out."

After dinner, Morgan headed to the bathroom to get ready for bed. She took out her toothbrush and ran it under the tap before squeezing some toothpaste on and starting to move it across her teeth in gentle circles.

Morgan finished brushing her teeth and ran the hairbrush gently through her hair, before making her way to bed.

...

Kipp waited impatiently in the cold morning air after knocking on Detective Carson's door. Her grimace from the cold disappeared the second the door opened. Carson looked unimpressed as she stared at Kipp. Morgan was behind her peering around the detective to look at Kipp.

"Hey! How's it going?" Kipp said, making sure to only make eye contact with Morgan.

"Ah, um, hey. What are you doing here?" Morgan asked, walking up next to the detective.

"Captain Brumbly told me that you got out yesterday, and I thought I'd swing by and say congrats," Kipp said as she rested her hand on her hip.

"He gave you my address?" Amelia questioned.

"...Yeah. Sorry, is this a bad time?"

"No, it's okay. Thank you." Morgan clasped her hands together as she struggled to make eye contact.

"Do you want to come in? We were about to have a snack."

"Sure!"

Kipp followed Morgan and the detective back to the table where there were apple slices and peanut butter waiting for them.

"Kipp, do you want something to drink?" Detective Carson asked.

"I'm okay, thanks," Kipp said, taking an apple slice and dipping it in the bowl of peanut butter.

"I have to go write some emails, but you guys feel free to take stuff from the fridge if you want more food." The detective got up from the table, taking a few slices with her as she headed to her office.

"Morgan?" Kipp said after the detective left the room.

"Yes?"

"I wanted to say sorry for the first time I met you. I kind of forgot that I was just supposed to be doing an interview and not an interrogation."

"Oh. It's okay," said Morgan.

"You know, you told me about you, but I've said nothing about me. I think you should ask me some questions."

"Okay," Morgan agreed. "I guess I'd want to ask about how you got so into the police investigation stuff."

"Well, my childhood was pretty normal for a while, but when I was eleven, my dad was killed in a car crash, and my mom was put in a coma because of it." Kipp went on, detailing how she started living with Nora and began taking self-defense classes with the captain. She tried to keep her tone neutral and face blank as she spoke. Morgan listened intently, leaning forward and face relaxed like Kipp's, but her eyes were open wider than normal. The car crash was by far the worst experience of her life, but the aftershock had taken its own toll. It took years for her to feel safe riding in a car again, and even now, she'd ride her bike whenever she could.

"What would happen before, when you tried to ride in a car?"

"Well, there was one time about two weeks after the crash." She looked out the window, not wanting to see Morgan's face as she described it. She'd been in the car with Nora on the way to the martial arts studio for a practice with Brumbly. She was explaining her then friend group's plan for a sleepover as Nora drove.

"...and we made a list of all the movies we're gonna watch, and we're gonna stay up all night!"

"That sounds like it's going to be fun. If you're going to stay up all night, hopefully you'll be able to sleep in for a while the next morning, otherwise you'll be out cold in your first class on Monday." Nora laughed.

"Yeah. I'll try to sleep in till like twelve," Kipp promised.

Nora continued down the road, only about a minute away from the studio, when a car pulled out in front of them. Nora slammed on the brakes, causing Kipp's body to slam against the seatbelt with the lurch of the car. Nora grunted, laying on the horn for a second in frustration.

"Sorry about that. That person pulled out in front of me," Nora said, letting out a nervous laugh. She glanced over at Kipp, whose hand was clutched onto the grab handle, her chest rising and falling with quick breaths. Kipp wanted to say something, but she didn't have the breath.

By the time Nora pulled into a parking spot at the studio, Kipp had calmed down enough to where her heart wasn't about to pound its way out of her chest.

"Are you okay? You seemed a little rattled back there."

"I'm okay now. I just got kind of scared we were going to crash," Kipp replied as she grabbed her bag from down at her feet. She only hoped the shaking in her legs would go away before she reached the door.

"That sounds scary. I'm sorry that happened," said Morgan.

"Yeah. It was a few days after my dad's funeral, so I think that kind of made it worse."

Her mother had bought her a new black dress to wear to the event. The short sleeves became uncomfortable once they walked into the cold funeral parlor.

Kipp had slowly walked through the sea of black fabric as she made her way to the armchair in the corner of the room. TVs lined the walls, showing pictures of her dad throughout his too short life. A picture appeared on the screen showing him holding a two-year-old Kipp on his shoulders. Kipp locked eyes with his smiling face, leaving her younger self in her peripheral vision. She ended up tearing away as she felt her chest heave with a longing for something that would never come. Her eyes met with the safety of the magenta carpet and did not leave until the last screen had gone black.

"I'm over it now, though," Kipp said quickly. "I don't have any problems with cars."

Morgan was silent for a few seconds.

"I'm sorry about your father," she said finally. "I didn't have a great relationship with my father, but I was still sad in a sense when he died, so I can't even imagine what it would've been like for you."

Kipp couldn't comprehend how Morgan could be sad when she was probably the one to kill her parents, but she didn't say anything about it. "It was pretty hard, but I'm all right now," she assured.

"That's good," said Morgan.

"It's kind of nice to talk to someone who actually…" Kipp broke eye contact. "Lost a parent. And at the same age, too. Like you said, obviously your whole situation is way different from mine, but it's still nice. A lot of people have dead grandparents and stuff, but losing an actual parent is pretty different."

"I agree. It's nice to talk to you too. Not just because of the shared experience, but just to talk to someone my age."

"I bet. Did you not really talk to the other people at the NJC?"

"No." Morgan looked down at the table, a smile spreading over her features. "You're kind of easier to talk to than them." She only made eye contact after she finished her sentence.

Kipp smiled, feeling her heart beat a little bit faster. "They must've been pretty awful for you to want to research drug dealers instead of talking to them."

"I'm sure some of them were okay. I just never took the time to get to know them. On the topic of drug dealers, I'm curious why Captain Brumbly got you involved in the Hall case."

"He just thought I'd think it was interesting. And I wanted to learn more about it. It kind of seems like Rundale has gone downhill since Hall brought in his unicorn dust. When I was on patrol with an officer, there was a break-in in this cute little neighborhood. A guy was trying to get money from someone he sold some unicorn dust to."

"The whole thing is pretty scary. I've tried to

distance myself from the case a little bit. It's hard with all the work I've done and the fact that the police are interviewing me and stuff, but I haven't done any research since the second note. I think Hall might have hacked Amelia's computer, or maybe one of the guards is working for Hall. Otherwise, I don't know how he knew I was involved."

Kipp nodded. She glanced at her phone, eyes widening as she saw a few texts from her mom, reminding her to lock the door if she left. She could have smacked herself in the head.

"Crap. I forgot to lock the door. I'm really sorry. I have to go." She threw her bag over her shoulder. "But I want to come over again sometime, if you're okay with that."

"Yeah, I'm— I'm okay with it," said Morgan.

"I'll see you soon, hopefully!"

While trying to finish a worksheet in stats, Kipp kept finding herself spacing out. Morgan's *smile* would not get out of her head. Every time the class would fall into a lull, Morgan was the first thing on her mind. It was a near foreign feeling, having her heart swell at the mere thought of someone. She felt like she would burst if she wasn't able to tell someone about it.

The next day, Kipp asked Nikki to talk in private after school.

"I think I might be interested in someone. Like,

romantically," Kipp confessed as she ran a hand through her hair.

"Ooh," Nikki teased, wiggling her eyebrows.

Kipp rolled her eyes. "When I tell you who it is, please don't freak out or anything, and also don't go around telling other people, at least not yet."

"You got it," Nikki promised.

"Okay." Kipp let out a breath. "You know that girl from the juvie center that I watched that interview of a while ago?"

Nikki's face scrunched in calm and collected confusion, but Kipp could see the shock in her eyes. "The murderer?"

Kipp let out a sigh at that word.

"I mean, yeah. But she didn't mean to kill that guy, and he was trying to hurt her, *and* she was twelve when it happened," she said.

Nikki opened her mouth to speak, but at first only blew out a breath of air. "You're sure she won't try to hurt you?"

"She wouldn't," Kipp muttered, barely loud enough for Nikki to hear.

"How do you know you like her? Like, have you talked to her? Besides the interview? Because if you're only going off looks—"

"I'm not. I've talked to her outside of interviews. She's a great person."

"As long as you're careful, then I support you," Nikki said, obviously putting effort into getting the words out. "What's her name again?"

Kipp forced a smile back onto her face. "Morgan."

"Right, right. Have you told her you like her?"

"No. Not yet. I thought I'd wait until we spent a little more time together. I feel like if I come on too strong I might scare her away or something, especially if she has no feelings toward me. And even if she didn't like me the same way, I'd still want to be friends."

"Yeah." Nikki cleared her throat. "I guess it'd be good to wait a little bit."

Kipp knew why Nikki was so unenthusiastic, but it still frustrated her that if Morgan was just about anyone else, Nikki would be fine with it. "I thought I'd try to see her again today."

"Good luck," Nikki said half-heartedly.

"Thanks, bye." Kipp waved as she grabbed her keys and jogged off to her car.

Before this, Kipp had never bothered with trying to get into a relationship. No one got her interested enough to want to pursue one. The farthest she got in discovering her romantic desires was coming to the conclusion she didn't like boys. Her full realization happened in freshman year, but there had been signs even when she was in sixth grade. The first time she'd really acknowledged it was at a sleepover with her old friend group— the night, they planned to watch movies until morning.

"Guys! We should play truth or dare!" Amanda, the host, exclaimed after the credits of the second movie began to roll.

"Yeah!" Nikki agreed.

"I'll go first," Chloe began, tightening her brown ponytail. "Adaline, truth or dare?"

"Um, truth," Adaline answered.

"Who do you like?" Chloe asked with a mischievous smile. Adaline rolled her eyes and scoffed playfully but didn't answer right away.

"Who is it?" Amanda pressed.

"Jackson!" Adaline blurted finally.

"Oh my gosh! I knew it!" Chloe giggled. "You're always trying to talk to him!"

"Yeah! And she stares at him all the time too," Nikki teased.

"Okay, okay, my turn," said Adaline. She hummed in deliberation, twirling a strawberry blonde strand of hair around her finger as she looked at the faces around her.

"Kipp. Truth or dare?"

"Dare," Kipp answered.

"I dare you to…" She took a second to think. "I dare you to prank call a random number."

"I don't have a phone, can I use yours?" Kipp asked.

"Fine," Adaline said. She tossed it over.

Dare was Kipp's answer over and over again. Unfortunately for her, it wasn't long before the girls started to protest.

"Aw, come on, Kipp. You have to pick truth at

some point," Nikki complained.

"Yeah. Truth or truth," Hannah asked with a falsely serious tone. Kipp laughed.

"Okay, fine. Truth."

"Who do you like?" Amanda asked, leaning forward with a smile as obnoxious as her hot pink silk pajamas.

Kipp quirked a brow. "I don't like anyone."

"Come on, just tell us," said Hannah, pulling on the hood of her koala onesie.

"No, I actually don't like anyone."

"There's so many boys at the school, you have to have at least a *little* crush on *one* of them," said Amanda.

"All the boys are weird. I wouldn't date any of them."

"Yeah but if you *had* to pick," said Chloe.

"I don't know! I just really don't like any of them," Kipp insisted, shrugging her shoulders. "Come on! Just pick *one*!" Adaline pushed.

"Guys, let's just move on. I'll go," Nikki stated, successfully taking some of the attention off of Kipp.

Nikki had always looked out for her like that. And Kipp knew that's what she was doing now with Morgan.

Kipp was sure Morgan wouldn't try to hurt her, but on the off chance she did, Kipp was sure she'd be able to defend herself. It felt almost shameful to think that Morgan would lash out like that. Her only other worry would be that she would fall head over heels for Morgan, only for Hall to end up hurting her. She let that thought leave her head as quickly as it had come.

Chapter 8

Morgan spent her time milling over schoolwork, waiting for Amelia to come home from the precinct. Kipp seemed so loving when she talked about her father. It made Morgan think of her own parents. She wanted to talk to them. To apologize and explain herself.

Finally, she heard the telltale click of the door and walked out of her bedroom to meet Amelia in the doorway.

"Hi, how was your day?" asked Morgan.

"It was good, thank you," said Amelia. "How was yours?"

"Good. I was wondering if we could drive over to Golden for a little bit."

"Sure. Why?"

"I, uh, want to visit my parents. To find some closure, I guess. I don't know exactly where they're buried, though… I didn't go to the funeral. I don't think there's a lot of cemeteries in Golden, but I don't want to go looking through all of them."

"I'm sure we can find the obituaries online, or maybe a news article that mentions where they are," the detective suggested as she pulled out her phone. "What are their names?"

"Adam and Deborah Toner."

"They are at…" Amelia drew out the last word as she scrolled through the search results. "Golden Memorial Cemetery. When do you want to visit?"

"Could we go today?"

"If you want to."

Morgan looked up from her feet as she heard a knock on the door. Amelia walked to the front of the house, Morgan following behind. Through the window beside the door, Morgan could see a familiar face on the other side.

"It's Kipp," said Amelia. "Do you want me to tell her to come back later?"

"No, it's okay," Morgan said as she stepped past the detective and pulled the door open.

"Hey, sorry to drop in, but I brought you guys some brownies," said Kipp. She held out a glass container that was covered by a rubber lid. "I don't bake a lot but I thought I'd bring you guys something since we had some brownie mix that probably wasn't going to be used for anything else." Kipp shrugged casually.

Morgan took the pan from Kipp. Her eyes glided along the sharpness of Kipp's jawline, the straightness of the bridge of her nose, moving up to rest on her dark eyes. She hadn't realized she forgot to respond until the detective spoke up.

"Thank you, that was very thoughtful. We were about to go on a little trip," said Amelia.

"Oh cool. Where to?" Kipp asked. The detective looked to Morgan, silently encouraging her to answer.

"Uh, Golden. I wanted to visit where my parents are." Morgan left out "buried," hoping Kipp would understand.

"Oh, okay. If this is a bad time, I can leave," Kipp offered, sticking her thumb up to gesture behind her.

"No, no. It's fine. You can come with us if you want."

"Are you sure? If you want to hang out or talk afterward, I can go home for now and you can call me when you're back."

"Really, it's okay. It might be nice to have someone else there."

They arrived at Golden Memorial Cemetery after an hour drive to find the area nearly empty, with only a few cars parked, and almost no one walking around. The ground was flat, with neat rows of headstones across it, some made out of rock that twinkled in the sunlight.

"Are you guys hungry? I can go into town and pick up some food," the detective offered once everyone parked their cars and got out.

"Yeah, that would be great, thank you!" Kipp said as she shut the door and locked her car.

Morgan stepped out of the passenger seat of the detective's car. "I am kind of hungry," she said.

Morgan and Kipp had no preference on what to eat, so Amelia set out to find something. "All right, I'll be back in twenty minutes at the latest," she said. "Kipp, I have your number, so I can text you right now so that you'll have mine. Call me if you need anything."

"Will do." Kipp waved as Amelia pulled out of the parking lot. She turned back to Morgan, who was staring blankly at the array of headstones and flowers poking out of the ground. "Do you want me to stay back?" she asked.

"Maybe for a little bit," Morgan said quietly. She walked past Kipp to the grass leading into the cemetery.

The grass contrasted with the dull gray of the gravestones. Small flowers had sprouted sparsely throughout the soft green blanket. Tiny daisies and buttercups bent under Morgan's shoes as she walked, searching for two familiar names engraved in stone. She clenched her jaw as she walked, as if she was preparing to speak to them rather than a chunk of rock. She hoped seeing the ground they were buried in would help her move on, to feel like she was actually looking them in the eyes, confronting them with her newfound freedom before offering an apology.

There were no other visitors that Morgan could see. That was, until she heard a familiar voice call out her name. Her stomach felt like it was free falling.

"I never thought we'd see you here," the voice drawled.

Kipp was leaning against her car scrolling through her phone when the sound of voices drew her attention. She craned her neck to see past a particularly large willow tree. Morgan was walking backward, and Kipp could see the fear in her eyes even from where she stood. She began curiously heading in Morgan's direction, but as soon as she saw that two people were quickly following after Morgan, she began to jog.

She could see them more clearly now. A man and a woman with stern faces. As she picked up her pace, Morgan's voice reached her on the breeze.

"Please just leave me alone! I don't want to talk to you," Morgan pleaded.

"You can't just come here to make amends or whatever you're here for, after what you've done."

"Who the hell are you?" Kipp cut in as she finally reached Morgan.

"I don't know who you are, but you need to stay out of this," the woman snapped.

"I'm her friend and—"

"And I'm her *aunt* and he's her *uncle*," the woman

said, accentuating the words by poking the air. "We have more of a right to talk to her than you do." With that, the woman turned away from Kipp, turning her attention back to her niece. Kipp stopped talking out of pure shock.

"You disobeyed them all the time. Deborah would call me every week to talk to me about how difficult you were being."

Kipp's stomach lurched seeing Morgan like this, with her hands clutched onto each other with white knuckles and her eyes filled with fear.

"I tried my best to listen, but no matter how hard I tried, I was never good enough for them!" Morgan's voice was breathy and quick.

"Of course you weren't good enough!" Morgan's uncle exclaimed. "You caused them so much stress."

"They would hit me all the time! If I spilled a little bit of food when setting the table, or didn't finish all my chores in time for dinner, I would end up with a bloody nose and a split lip."

Kipp prepared to watch Morgan's relatives pause in shock, taking in what she had just said with a bit of sympathy, but their faces remained unchanged.

"They were trying to make sure you became a functioning young lady in this world, and *you* disobeyed them," said Morgan's uncle. "Their discipline choices weren't a reason to disrespect them like you did. They only wanted what was best for you, but oh no, you wanted to be wild and not listen to a thing they said."

"I tried," Morgan said helplessly, her voice breaking into a sob at the end. Kipp could now see tears gathering in Morgan's eyes, about to spill over.

"You're a pathetic excuse for a daughter. Worse than an embarrassment. And what did you end up as after your parents weren't there to straighten you out? A delinquent."

"Shut the fuck up!" Kipp's voice burst from her throat.

"Excuse me?" Morgan's uncle sneered, his eyes wide with shock.

"I said shut the fuck up," she growled, taking a threatening step forward.

"As my wife *clearly* said: this doesn't concern you. We are her family, and we have a right to—"

"You aren't her family. You don't deserve her. Her parents beat the shit out of her every day and you're *defending* them? If you think you're good people while you're making excuses for child abusers, and calling your own niece an embarrassment for not wanting to be *abused*, you are a different kind of fucked up. Morgan is amazing. She's smart, she's kind, she's beautiful, and *apparently* you can't see that. Go back to whatever hell hole you crawled out of." The couple stood in stunned silence as Kipp curled an arm around Morgan's back, guiding her away. Morgan's tears were quick to resume flowing, although not for the same reason. "I'll call Detective

Carson so we can meet up with her," Kipp said as they reached the car. She opened the passenger door for Morgan to climb inside. "Man, some people are awful." Her eyes stopped on Morgan, but she didn't say anything, just stared.

"Can we go now?" Morgan asked.

"Oh yeah, yeah, of course. I'll call Amelia right now." Kipp rounded the car, slid into the driver's seat, and quickly started the engine. "Don't forget your seatbelt," she said as they began pulling out of the parking lot. Morgan obliged, clicking the metal into place. "And if you want to talk about anything, I'm here."

They drove in silence after that.

"Are you okay? Did something happen?" The detective rushed over with her bag of takeout to where Kipp had just gotten out of her car. Kipp made no effort to lift her face out of its resting position, which she guessed was why Carson got concerned. Morgan looked more dazed than anything, looking out the car window at the sidewalk.

"These two people that said they were Morgan's aunt and uncle started harassing her."

"Oh my God. I'm sorry I wasn't there. But you're okay, right? No one got hurt?"

"No. They yelled a lot, but they didn't hurt us."

"I'm sorry that happened. Do you want some food?" she grabbed a container from the bag, offering it to Morgan through the open car window. Morgan nodded and took the bag.

"Can we go home?" she asked meekly.

"Definitely. Kipp, are you okay to drive back? Like, to your house?"

"Yeah." Kipp's face was soft and understanding as she looked back to Morgan, who was shifting around nervously, her eyes constantly scanning the street. Amelia followed Kipp's gaze.

"Morgan and I should probably hurry up and go. Here's your food." She handed a triangular container from the bag of food to Kipp. "I hope you like pizza."

Kipp did like pizza. She took the box, thanking Detective Carson. As Kipp was saying her goodbyes, Morgan stuck her head out the window.

"And thanks for uh, talking to my aunt and uncle for me," she called.

"Any time!" Kipp responded. She never wanted to see Morgan like that again. It had been painful to watch her lip quiver as she shrank into herself. Kipp wanted to protect her somehow, to stand between her and anything that wished to do her harm.

Kipp's thoughts were dominated by Morgan's past, but they eventually shifted to the future. She wanted to get to know Morgan. To really *know* her. "Hey!" she called, running up to the detective's car. Morgan turned around to look through the window again. "Would you want to go on a walk with me tomorrow?" Kipp asked.

"Sure! What, uh, what time?" asked Morgan.

Kipp couldn't help smiling in relief. "How about three? I can meet you at Detective Carson's house. There's a cafe with really good pastries near there."

"That sounds great." Morgan's voice was brighter than ever. "I'll see you tomorrow!"

Kipp slid into the driver's seat of her car, sighing. *I really hope I didn't make her uncomfortable yelling at her relatives. Maybe I should've just got her to walk away with me. What if it made her way more stressed that I started arguing with them? Ugh, and I called her beautiful. Let's just hope that wasn't going too far. At least she agreed to the walk.*

Morgan's knees threatened to turn to jelly as she felt the wash of relief stepping into Amelia's house. She sank into the bouncy cushions of the couch, letting herself be embraced by the calming scent of the vanilla air freshener plugged into the nearby outlet. Her aunt and uncle's words were still unrelenting in her head, and a sudden thought turned her relief to be back home into dread.

"What if they try to take custody of me or something? Would we be able to get evidence that they aren't suited to be parents?"

"Don't worry about that," Amelia assured. "I'm not going to let that happen. If they try to take you, or hurt you in any way, they're going to have me to deal with."

Kipp arrived home, still clenching her jaw every time the faces of Morgan's aunt and uncle jumped into her mind. If Morgan's parents had been even half as bad as her aunt and uncle, Kipp couldn't imagine how she'd spent eleven years with them.

The next day, Kipp rushed to her closet, bouncing on her toes as she wracked her brain for something to wear. *A suit? Hell no. No one wears a suit to a casual walk. Maybe a collared shirt and corduroys? No, still too formal. T-shirt and jeans? But what if she wears something more formal? Eh, she probably won't. I should probably wear a jacket or something. Do any of my flannels even match my shirts?*

Kipp eventually settled for gray jeans, a white graphic t-shirt and her favorite red flannel. The detective's house was only a few miles away, but Kipp had to drive to avoid the freezing March wind. She got into the car and started it, doing a quick test to make sure the horn and brakes worked before wrapping her hands tightly around the wheel.

The house had off-white wood constructing the outside, and reddish tiles over the roof. A few small bushes lined the sidewalk leading to the detective's door.

After only one ring of the doorbell, the door swung open and Morgan stepped out onto the porch. Kipp had known this girl for barely over a week, yet her stomach swooped at the sight. Morgan had in fact worn a casual outfit: a plain, white sweatshirt and loose-fitting light blue jeans.

"Are you ready to go?" Yeah." Morgan smiled. "How far is the cafe?"

"It's up the road a few blocks and across the street. I go there with my friends a lot. It's called Cafe Roxy."

"I think I've seen it before, but I've never tried anything from there."

"They have a lot of different stuff. They have coffee stuff and pastries obviously, but they also serve breakfast and lunch. They make really good smoked salmon."

"I'm not really in the mood for fish, but I'll have to try it sometime," said Morgan. She stuffed her hands in her pockets as her fingers started to become stiff from the cold.

It was a relief to step inside the warm cafe. Morgan took her hands out of her pockets, starting to huff hot air onto them and grasp her fingers to warm them up. She studied the menu, which was displayed on blackboards in colorful chalk on the wall behind the counter.

"What do you think you're going to get?" asked Kipp.

"Maybe a raspberry danish?" Morgan had meant

it as an answer, but it definitely came out more like a question. Around everyone, even Amelia, she felt the need to be decisive. When she couldn't put on a confident face, the least she could do was deliver forceful answers. But it was different with Kipp. Morgan felt nervous around her to the point where she questioned almost any action she took.

"Cool." Kipp waited a few seconds. "Is that what you want or are you still thinking?"

"Yeah, sorry. I'll get the raspberry danish."

"No, you're fine, I just wanted to make sure." Kipp walked up to the counter and gave the cashier their order.

The smell of the pastries spread through the front of the cafe as they were heated up.

A few minutes later, the two sat down at one of the tables to eat the warm pastries. Kipp took the muffin out of the bag and unwrapped it before taking a big bite out of the top. The outing seemed to be going well so far, but a chill was sneaking its way into Morgan's bones.

As Kipp happily popped the last bite in her mouth, she looked over to see that Morgan had only eaten about half of hers. Her teeth had begun to chatter, and she was shivering.

"Are you cold?" Kipp asked. Morgan exhaled something close to a laugh.

"Yes. I probably should've worn more layers," she said, taking a few more bites of her danish.

"They usually have the air conditioning on in here. Even in winter. It feels nice when you first get in because it's warmer than outside, but after a while you can kind of tell it's not actually that warm," said Kipp. She crumpled the wax paper bag with the muffin wrapper inside and tucked it into her pocket. "Do you want to go back to Amelia's? It'll be cold walking back, but if you're super uncomfortable in here…"

"No, it's okay." Morgan turned back to her food, continuing to take tiny nibbles.

"All right," Kipp said, clearly unconvinced, but Morgan only smiled and kept eating.

"I'm okay. I'll probably feel better in a little bit."

"Maybe I could warm you up," Kipp offered with a sunny smile. Morgan turned her head to look at Kipp, her brows raised in silent question. "I mean, you know, if we sat a little closer together, body heat would probably help."

"Probably," Morgan mumbled as she slid closer, leaving a few inches between them. She felt her cheeks heat up when Kipp put her arm around her and pulled her closer. Morgan leaned further into the hold, covering her smile with what was left of her danish as her heart thrummed with happiness. Even after she finished the pastry, Morgan still held the bag up to her mouth as if she was still eating, not wanting to move just yet.

She eventually set the bag in her lap, prepared to

immediately pull away, or stay put based on Kipp's reaction. Although she would have been content staying cuddled up to Kipp for hours, she wouldn't tell her that in case it came off as weird, and of course she didn't want to pull away and risk Kipp thinking she didn't like it.

Kipp did not move when she heard the crinkle of Morgan putting the empty bag down.

"How was the danish?" Kipp asked.

"It was good. How was your muffin?"

"Good."

"Do you come here often?" Morgan bit the inside of her cheek.

"Yeah, I go with my friends a lot. A lot of places have closed recently, so hopefully this won't."

"Uh huh."

It was silent for a few moments.

"Are you ready to go?" Kipp asked eventually.

"Yeah," said Morgan. She got up rather quickly, not wanting to overstay her welcome in Kipp's arms.

"Are you a little warmer now?"

"Yes. That helped a lot."

"Good. Hopefully we can speed walk back to Detective Carson's so you aren't frozen again by the time we get there." Kipp held the door for Morgan to walk through into the cold.

With every step on the way back, Morgan became more and more conflicted. *I* really *like her. But what if she doesn't like me? She seems like she does… Even if she does, she shouldn't have to deal with me. I cry all the time, I'm a damn* murderer, *I wouldn't know how to sustain a relationship to save my life, and on top of all that, Hall is after me…* She drew her arms around herself. *But she makes me* happy. *God, why do I have to be so selfish?*

"I'll see you later?" Kipp interrupted her thoughts. She was pulled back to the present, where they had reached Detective Carson's front door.

"Um, yeah, maybe," Morgan managed, before stepping forward and opening the door, giving Kipp an awkward smile as she shut it.

The same blissful smile she had at the cafe would have stayed on Kipp's face all day if it weren't for that last thing Morgan had said. *She looked happy at the cafe, though. It's fine, I'm probably overthinking it.*

She called the detective's phone twice that day. The first time she called it went to voicemail. The second time, the detective answered, saying that Morgan was busy. It was understandable, something Kipp could brush off. It was a little less dismissible when three days had passed and Kipp still hadn't been able to interact with Morgan.

On Monday, Kipp walked into prom committee knowing she wouldn't be able to pay attention. She kept her eyes on the speaker, but her mind never ceased to wander. Had she made Morgan uncomfortable? Maybe Morgan only wanted to be friends and she had pushed too far. Should she go to the detective's house and check?

"Kipp? You've been pretty quiet so far. Do you want to add anything?" a teacher asked.

"Uh, yeah. I think the theme is good, and for the decorations I think we should add some

decorations with light green instead of just dark," Kipp answered. She wanted to ask Morgan to prom, but the recent events were making her worried that chance had gone out the window. She had to take some kind of action toward talking to her.

That afternoon, she went to the detective's house, hoping to talk.

Kipp had never been one to nervously fidget, but she found herself playing with the zipper on her jacket, not wanting to look up from the wood boards of the porch. Her head shot up as the door swished open. Morgan kept her hand on the handle.

"Are we good? Did I make you uncomfortable, or mad or something? You've seemed like you really don't want to talk to me for the past few days." Kipp talked faster than she was already planning to, afraid Morgan would slam the door.

"No, I'm fine." Morgan's voice was flat, and she avoided eye contact as she went to step back into the house.

Kipp stuck her foot in the door, keeping it from closing. "Wait! Do you not want to be friends or, you know, like, anything else? I thought you did, but maybe I was wrong. Was I wrong?"

At those words, Morgan stopped attempting to pull the door closed. She swallowed, looking at the sidewalk, as she struggled to push her answer past her lips, but her unsaid words were clear to Kipp.

"You could've said something earlier, you know. Why did you think ignoring me for five days was a better idea than just saying something?"

"I don't know," Morgan forced out.

"Well, I hope you can figure it out at some point, because it wasn't very fun for me," Kipp snapped. She fought the urge to look back as she walked away.

Her eyes glowed amber with the light of the setting sun, making the tears glossing over them all the more obvious. As she placed her hand on the stick shift to put her car in drive, she hesitated, finally looking back to the door to the detective's house, but it was already closed.

On her drive home she strained to keep her eyes dry, occasionally banging her hands against the steering wheel. She nearly swerved into the other lane as tears blurred her vision. Only a single droplet was able to escape, and even then it was vigorously brushed away.

Morgan shut herself in her room, and sat on the bed, deciding it would be pointless to try and wipe away the endless flow of tears. *This is what I wanted, right? But it's not* really. *Am I being selfish? What's* wrong *with me? Now she's never going to want to talk to me ever again.*

Hot tears streamed down Morgan's face as her thoughts dissolved into regret, longing settling in her bones. As Kipp had walked off, Morgan had stared back at her, silently begging her to turn around and come back to ask her why one more time, and then maybe— *No. She doesn't deserve the chaos I would bring into her life,* she had thought.

At least Kipp wouldn't have to deal with her anymore. She wrapped her arms tightly around her torso in some pitiful attempt to hold herself together as sobs wracked her body, causing her to double over. She began to cry harder as she realized no matter how tightly she curled her arms around herself, it wouldn't satisfy the ache she felt in her chest: a pain that could so simply have been diminished by a single hug.

She eventually calmed down enough to allow the redness to leave her eyes.

Detective Carson returned a few hours later while Morgan was sitting on the living room couch.

"Hey, how was your day?" she asked, sitting down in an armchair.

"Good," said Morgan.

"Did Kipp ever stop by? She called a few times."

"No."

"Huh. That's weird. She really seemed like she

wanted to talk to you. Maybe something came up. And remember, you don't have to talk to her if you don't want to."

"I know," Morgan assured.

"Hey, I was thinking about booking you some therapy sessions. I think it would be a good idea."

"Would it be like going to the psychiatrist at the juvenile center?"

"No. I'd make sure to find you a really good therapist that is really going to work to help you and make you feel like you're in a safe environment."

"But isn't it really expensive?"

"I'll be worth it if you're going to benefit from it. Do you think you'd want to try it out?"

Morgan looked up at a speck on the ceiling as she considered it. It would probably be good for her to talk about some of the stuff that had happened to her, but how could she trust a complete stranger with even a word of her past? "Maybe later in life, but I don't think it would be helpful right now to talk to someone I've never met before about what happened to me."

"Okay. Let me know if you change your mind." Amelia leaned back in her chair. "And if you want to talk to someone you know, I'll always be free for a conversation, or to just listen."

Morgan nodded. Just knowing she had someone to talk to now was enough.

Kipp was glad her mother wasn't home when she arrived back, otherwise Roberta would've heard it when she slammed her bedroom door and drove her fist into the nearest wall. Unsurprisingly, it didn't make her feel better. It just pointlessly added to her pain.

Damn it, you should've gone back. You probably fucking scared her with how aggressive you were being. I guess you'll have to get over it since you clearly fucked everything up. Kipp drew in a deep breath and looked to the ceiling as she felt her eyes grow hot once more. *Okay, well, maybe it wouldn't have worked out even if I did absolutely everything right. Either way, I'm going to have to get over her one way or another.* She dug her fingernails into her palms when the tears were close to falling over her lash line. *But the least she could've done was tell me why she wanted to avoid me, instead of just not talking to me at all. Maybe she was scared? She still could've said something. Or asked Carson to say something*. She leaned forward, letting gravity pull her to collapse on her bed.

When Kipp opened her eyes the next morning, they still had the sting of tiredness in them, as if she hadn't slept at all. She rolled out of bed, her back popping as she twisted around.

Opting for a glass of water for breakfast, Kipp quickly headed for the door, hoping her mom was too busy to strike up a conversation that morning.

"Bye! Have a good day!" her mother called.

"Bye," said Kipp. The door shut.

When she arrived at school, Isabel and Luke were sitting on the front steps. Isabel's black eyes were shining with a level of excitement that was too high for this early in the morning as she talked to Luke. She was telling him about how opossums make great pets and that it was extremely rare for them to get rabies. All of them normally got to school at least a few minutes before it started, save for Nikki, who slept right up until the last second and still arrived at school barely on time.

"Hey!" Isabel greeted. Luke waved and they both stood up as Kipp approached.

"Did you guys decide on a theme for prom yet?" Luke asked.

"Yeah. Magic forest," Kipp droned.

"You don't sound very happy about that."

"I mean, it's fine, I guess." Kipp shrugged.

"I can't wait!" said Isabel. "It's going to be so fun! We should all go shopping together."

"Yeah. I heard about this really cool formalwear outlet in Denver. How about we go there to pick stuff out?" Luke suggested.

"Cool," said Kipp. She tried her best to keep her eyes wide and the corners of her mouth upturned, hoping to avoid any questions about how she was doing.

"By the way, not to brag or anything but..." Luke

paused for effect "I got into NC State! I was on the waitlist for a while, but I finally got in!"

"Yo, congrats! We're all going to have to have, like, a weekly Skype meeting or something to stay in touch," Kipp said with an almost entirely genuine smile. She glanced around, noticing a certain absence. "Where's Nikki?"

"She's probably late. She FaceTimed the group chat at like one a.m. to say she didn't get into her top school, but got her second choice."

"Oh. Huh. I mean, at least she got her second choice." Kipp released the tension from her shoulders as the attention remained off of her.

"Yeah, she sounded pretty happy about it."

"Why were you up at one in the morning? I thought you had a quiz today," said Isabel.

"I'm running on coffee." Luke shook the thermos in his hand. "I'll be fine. Hey, homeroom starts in like two minutes. We should probably go."

"I'll see you guys later!" Isabel hauled her backpack onto her shoulders and hurried inside, having to pull her dark hair out from under the strap on the way.

"Hey, you good?" Luke asked quietly as Kipp started walking to the door.

"Yeah. I'm just kind of tired." Kipp smiled again, hoping he couldn't tell it wasn't real.

Kipp found herself looking at her phone at every water break during her lacrosse practice. There was no sun beating down on them that day, yet her face was tinged with a permanent shade of pink.

As the team continued warm-ups, she carefully caught the ball in the cradle of her stick, rearing to toss it back to her partner. The ball whizzed through the air and hit her teammate in the shoulder. The girl let out an *oof* sound before scooping the ball up off the ground.

"My bad," Kipp called.

"You're good," the girl said.

Kipp dragged a hand across her face. Hopefully the rest of practice wouldn't go as badly as warmups.

The team gathered in center field as the coach called them over.

"All right, everybody warmed up? Good. Like we talked about yesterday, we're going to have a scrimmage. I'm going to split you up into two teams. If I send you to the right, you put on a green penny, left puts on the yellow ones."

They were broken into groups, Kipp raising her brows at a teammate as they put on the surely unwashed pennies. Luckily, the smell wasn't that noticeable after the game had started. The ball was passed to Kipp, and she began running. She zig-zagged around the defenders, keeping her eyes stuck on the right side of the goal where there was a gap between the goalie and the edge of the goal. Another player blocked her path, causing her to stop a few yards from her target. She caught sight of a fellow green penny running to free herself for a pass. Kipp threw the ball, relaxing a bit as the person who had previously been guarding her backed off. She sucked air in through her teeth as she watched the ball fly far out of her teammates reach, landing on the ground for the other team to pick up.

"Kipp! Easy on the throw! We don't have that long until the next game, and we can't afford to have you doing that in the middle of it!" her coach yelled from the sidelines. Kipp twisted her foot into the grass as she acknowledged her coach with a nod. She gripped her stick tighter as her cheeks turned even redder with embarrassment.

"Hey! How was school?" her mom asked when she got home.

"Good," Kipp said. Her mom waited for a while, but Kipp didn't elaborate, just continued to untie her shoes.

"Did you have a bad day?" asked Roberta.

"No."

"Okay, I just wanted to check, because you seem like you're on a pretty short fuse. You kind of seemed like that this morning, and you do now. Did something happen yesterday?"

"No, I'm just tired."

"Well, if you need to talk about something, I'll be here."

"I know," Kipp sighed. "I'm going to the precinct.

I told Captain Brumbly I would stop by to help program and box the body cams. I'll probably be back before eight."

"Text me when you're about to leave so I can warm you up some food."

"I will." Kipp took her wallet and keys out of her backpack and walked out the door.

The temperature outside was dropping fast when she finally found the captain. He was in one of the meeting rooms, having opened one of the three boxes that were sitting on the table.

"There you are," said the captain. "I was getting worried because I realized I forgot to tell you what room we'd be in."

"It's fine." Kipp walked over to the opened box and started grabbing the smaller boxes that contained the cameras from inside.

"These are new, so we're going to have to put them in those little charging stations over there." He pointed to some black cradles with blinking lights that were plugged into the wall. "When the cameras are unboxed, we'll slide them into the charging station and they'll beep when they're done. When they're charged, make sure to turn them off, and then put them back in the box."

Working at the precinct was always relaxing, especially when Kipp was in a bad mood. She'd never had to deal with anyone asking how she was feeling.

"Got it. Is there any new stuff with the Hall case?"

Kipp asked.

"Well, it looks like he's escalating. The Boulder police were monitoring a man that they thought could be involved in the drug ring, and this afternoon he, his wife, and their house cleaner were found shot in their home, and red casings were on the ground. No one knew about it until the wife's boss called in a wellness check when she didn't show up for work."

"Do they know how the wife and cleaner were involved?"

"Hall has no qualms about killing innocents."

Kipp's mind jumped to Morgan. The box she was picking up slipped from her hands.

"Whoops." She smiled. Kipp opened her mouth to ask for more details about what he meant by that, but nothing came out. She set the box on the table, working up the nerve to try her question again. "So, he—" Her voice cracked. "So he could still be trying to hurt Morgan Toner even when she stopped researching the case."

"Definitely. He could be coming after her just to make a point."

Kipp continued to unbox the cameras, ignoring the way her chest twisted like a wind up toy.

The leftovers of Morgan's sorrow weighed her down as she walked through the empty streets of Rundale, past closed businesses and the occasional old house with an overgrown lawn. It had been a day since she last saw Kipp. Morgan expected to feel better about her decision by now, but nothing had changed.

She stopped at a bench, slouching as she sat down. She had told Amelia that she had been feeling a little down lately, although she didn't say why. Amelia suggested a few things that could make her feel better: ice cream, a funny movie, a puzzle, a walk, etcetera. Morgan thought it might be nice to go on a walk if she really bundled up, but all it did was make her think of the walk to and from the cafe with Kipp.

Just then, she saw a familiar face walking down the street. Kipp wore a solemn expression, and was hunched over as she made her way down the sidewalk, her hands shoved in her pockets. Morgan swallowed as she realized she was only a block away from the police department.

All thoughts left her head as they made eye contact. Not knowing what to do, she just stared. She broke her gaze away, tears threatening to fill her eyes. Kipp started running to her as Morgan began briskly walking away.

"Hey! The least you can do is tell me why you were avoiding me. Was I annoying or something? I want to know," Kipp pushed.

Morgan gritted her teeth, struggling with choosing an answer.

"Please tell me," Kipp continued. "I really liked you, and I thought you felt the same, but even though you don't, that doesn't mean you can just ignore me."

"I'm sorry. I didn't… It's just, I'm not a good person. You don't deserve to be with someone who's taken away another human's life. And I'd probably be really high maintenance and—"

"*That's* why? Because you thought you weren't *good enough* for me? I thought I made it pretty clear that I didn't think that."

"But you should! You're wonderful, and I'm just not!"

"You *accidentally* killed one guy that tried to assault you," Kipp said, lowering her voice. "And if you did kill your parents…" Her expression was soft and sympathetic as she leaned closer to Morgan. "I think that's forgivable. They hurt you every day. They made your life hell, and you *still* feel really bad about it."

Forgivable. The word bounced loudly across the walls of Morgan's mind.

"You don't understand. It wasn't just them. There was this girl, Grace, that would bully me, and was the reason my friend Serena moved, and I—"

"Morgan! Stop! You—" Kipp began making a gesture with her hand, quickly raising it in the air. She cut herself off as Morgan *flinched*, throwing her hands up in a defensive motion.

Silence enveloped the world around them as Kipp slowly brought her hand down, her own breath roaring in her ears. "I'm— I'm sorry. I wasn't going to hit you. I swear, I would never."

Morgan only stared at her, lip still quivering.

Kipp immediately dropped her arm back to her side.

"I would never hit you. You know that right?" Her brows knitted together as she fought the urge to pull Morgan into a hug, to show her she cared somehow, to do *anything* to quell the fear in her eyes.

"What— But what if I tried to hurt you?" Morgan uttered, voice as slight as a feather.

"Honestly, if you were trying to hurt me, I'd probably deserve it." Kipp tried her best to crack a smile. Morgan did not reciprocate the effort. Kipp dropped the awkward attempted grin and continued. "What were you even saying about that girl Grace? Did you hurt her?"

Morgan didn't answer.

"Morgan." Kipp said. "What did you do?"

Chapter 9

Five years ago

The back door slammed behind Morgan as she took off into the patch of woods behind the house to her favorite tree. Just last year, she had made a sort of platform which was a collection of large sticks strategically placed between branches, and in the dark it was impossible to see unless you knew exactly where to look. It had no ladder leading to it, and though it supported Morgan's weight, it was really just a pile of sticks, so even if someone saw it, there was a chance they would ignore it.

Morgan climbed up the tree and hung the backpack she brought with her on a branch. Not long after she caught her breath, she heard police sirens in the distance, inevitably coming to her house where they would find her parents' bodies. Later, a few officers came into the woods, their flashlights dancing through the trees, but never landing on the shivering girl perched in one of them. When the officers returned to the house having found nothing, Morgan finally allowed sleep to consume her.

The pleasant song of birds played through the trees, a tune far too happy for Morgan's liking as she woke up. Her sweatshirt was stiff with dried blood and her back was sore. She judged it was about eight in the morning. She'd probably gotten, at most, two hours of sleep with how many times she woke up in the night. She shifted around so that she could unzip her backpack and pull out a granola bar. The wrapper crinkled as she tore it open.

After finishing the bar, she started grabbing handfuls of her hoodie, trying to get it to loosen up. *What am I going to do? We don't have security cameras, but my blood dripped everywhere. I can probably tell the police someone else killed them and then scratched my face before I ran away. If I get rid of the knife and pen, that could work. Maybe the foster system won't be that bad. If I can convince them I need to go there instead of a relative's.* She stuffed the knife that was lying beside her into her backpack, threw it over her shoulder and climbed down from the tree. While walking, she spit onto her sleeve and rubbed it over her face to get the blood spatters off, making sure to drag her feet in the dirt to cover up the blood on her shoes. She eventually came to the running trail that connected to another part of her neighborhood. Examining herself, she let out a breath as she found the dark clothing concealed the blood well. With that, she walked out into the sunlight.

Before Grace had cut off her hair, it had come down to her waist, usually in pretty braids or ponytails, and now it was a little above her shoulders. Her parents never posted pictures of her on social media, and she looked different enough from the few pictures they had of her in the house. She passed a few people on the sidewalk, anticipating someone would recognize her, but no one did. Morgan had only gone to Denver twice, but she figured that was where she would go, since not many people would know her there.

She caught the first bus she could. The medical tape on her face earned her some odd stares, but no one said anything.

After getting off at the first stop in Denver and walking for a while, Morgan felt a wave of grief hit her. *Why am I sad? I did it for my own good.*

It wasn't the only way. Morgan pondered every possible thing she could have done differently. Waiting it out until she was eighteen, calling child protective services, running away, becoming a complete and utter disappointment to her parents and hoping they disowned her rather than beat her within an inch of her life. To her frustration, no matter how many ideas came to mind, the past still stayed the same.

Why did I do that? I'm going to go to prison and I'll

probably get assaulted and abused and it won't be any better than at home. It might even be worse. What was I thinking*? Why couldn't I have waited it out until I was eighteen?*

Calm down. *They* deserved *it. They deserved it.*

She stopped and sat down on a bus stop bench. *I've been walking for so long. No one has noticed me yet. Come to think of it, there's only one person here who would know who I am. Grace.*

It's all her fault! If she hadn't made Serena move away, I would've still had a friend to talk to, and I would've waited my parents out and I never would have killed them. As vengefulness took over once more, Morgan pulled on her hoodie, and began walking to look for the address Grace had always bragged about.

Morgan walked through alleyways, across streets, until she came to a large house with *Monroe* printed in cursive on the mailbox. *Of course. The fanciest one.* Morgan pushed her hair back into the hood and pulled it over her face. She grabbed the knife from her backpack and quickly tucked the blade into the pocket of her hoodie. Her eyelid twitched from exhaustion as she pulled on the gloves that she had stuffed in her backpack. Then, she continued down the street until she was out of sight from all the windows.

She rounded the house, staying hidden behind the row of large bushes that separated the neighboring house from Grace's. Her breathing quickened as she saw that their patio door was cracked open. Morgan approached it from the side, creeping along the wall so she could dodge the gaze of the security cameras. There was only one that was unavoidable, but she cut her losses and covered her face with her hood, figuring there'd be cameras inside too.

She ducked into the house through the cracked door, making sure not to bump it in case it squeaked, but hesitated before touching her foot to the floor. Her teeth clenched when she looked at her filthy shoes. She ended up sliding them off and putting them in her backpack, which she shoved behind a potted plant right outside the door. Stepping through the house in her socks, Morgan became more comfortable, tiptoeing around the house and looking into rooms. They were all perfectly clean with expensive looking furniture and art. Her body had started to sway as she walked, making it harder to be quiet and avoid bumping into anything. She always kept her head down and her hood pulled over her face.

By the time she moved upstairs, it was clear there was no one home. Morgan peeked into Grace's room— her name was spelled out in wooden letters hanging laterally on the wall. A cloud of mixed perfumes hit her like a slap in the face when she walked in. She went into the walk-in closet and hid behind the door, all the while keeping her shirt pulled over her nose.

She had no idea how long she sat in that closet, trying not to fall asleep against the wall. It could have been thirty minutes or three hours for all she knew.

Then, Morgan's heart sped up as she heard two muffled voices from downstairs.

"Grace, could you please make sure to close and lock the door next time? Someone could have gotten in."

"Well *sorry* I forget things sometimes."

Morgan heard footsteps coming up the stairs. She nearly flinched as the door to the bedroom flew open and shut just as quickly. Grace strode into her room, talking on her phone.

"I know! I didn't see them anywhere!" she said. Morgan felt her chest constrict. "Yeah! I bet they both moved or something. Neither of them can take a joke. Serena always yells and stuff, and then Morgan will just bawl her eyes out if I look at her wrong." Grace laughed, blissfully unaware that the sound rang in the ears of the very person she was speaking of, igniting anger that Morgan felt would explode out of her any second. She could barely feel her hand gripping the knife in her pocket.

Grace passed the closet, starting to talk about something completely different, as if Serena and Morgan were no more important to her than the dirt on the bottom of her shoes. Morgan's anger peaked. She took a step out from behind the closet door, but upon hearing the bedroom door open, she quickly moved back into the shadows.

"Hi, sweetie, if you need anything, we'll be in our bedroom watching some shows," Grace's mother said.

"I know," Grace said loudly, clearly annoyed. "Can you see that I'm talking to someone right now?"

"Sorry, I didn't mean to interrupt," her mother said with an undertone of sadness in her voice. The door quietly closed. Grace scoffed, continuing to pace around the room on her phone. Morgan pulled her hand out of her pocket, realizing she had nicked her finger on the blade. Her mind wandered to what the aftermath of Grace's death would look like. Her parents would have to bury their child, Morgan could be caught, Grace might have turned out nicer in adulthood. *I can't, I can't, I can't.*

What am I doing?

Morgan dug her teeth into her lip, a wave of panic quickly washing over her. *How am I going to get out?* She moved completely behind the door. Stress sloshed in her stomach and chest. She dragged her nails across her hands and face, trying to quell it.

"Yeah, hold on," Grace said into the phone. Morgan heard the covers crinkle as Grace got up from her bed. "Mom! I'm hungry."

Morgan heard a voice come from another room. "Do you want me to make you a snack?"

"I wouldn't be telling you I'm hungry if I didn't," Grace said back.

"Okay, what do you want?"

"I don't know. Something good."

"Well, last time I made you something you didn't like. Could you please tell me what you want?"

Grace groaned, opening the door and walking out of her room.

"What do we have?" she said, voice getting more muffled. Grace's mother began listing off snack ideas. Quickly shifting her weight between her feet, Morgan peered out of the closet at the empty bedroom before stepping out. There were two windows, and neither looked like they had screens. She debated picking up the small tuffet that sat in front of Grace's desk, but decided it would take too much time.

She fumbled to get the window open. Her gloves made it difficult to get the small, stubborn lock to slide to the side. As soon as it moved to the right, Morgan rushed to pull the window open. She looked out to estimate the drop. There was nothing but a few bushes to cushion her fall if she were to jump, so she decided to try to climb as low as she could until she inevitably slipped. She climbed out head first, turning around and resting her knees on the sill so she could pull the window shut again.

Once she lowered herself down, desperately gripping the sill with her hands, it was clear that she should have risked taking off her gloves. Morgan's grasp immediately slipped once her full weight was hanging from the window. Air rushed past her clothes and her stomach seemed to float for a second.

The bushes' spiny branches hit her back with a *swish*, and the leaves prodded at her through her clothes like needles. She stifled a whimper and rolled off onto the soft grass, then ran along the side of the house. She snatched her bag off the ground and bolted for the bushes dividing the two yards with her backpack held to her chest.

She made it to another street by running down the line of hedging and fences that separated houses. Before walking onto the sidewalk, she pulled down her hood and put on an extra jacket from her backpack.

Morgan walked slowly up the street with a blank face. *How did it come to this?* Her thoughts were pulled back to reality as hunger started to claw at her stomach. She could see the tall buildings of the city center in the distance and decided that would be her best bet to find food.

Eventually she saw a Wendy's a short distance away. Taking off her gloves, she hurried across the street and entered the building. She pulled a few single dollar bills out of the front pocket of her backpack, money that she'd stolen from her father's wallet before leaving home.

Approaching the counter with as much confidence as she could, she ordered a burger and a water. She went to the drink station, filling up a cup of water before sliding into a booth and unwrapping her food.

She stared at the burger in contemplation of whether her meager savings were worth this, but quickly took a bite as her stomach began to cramp.

Half the burger had made it into her stomach when Morgan heard sirens in the distance that were getting louder. She turned around to see two police cars racing down the road. She casually turned back around and resumed eating.

Morgan sat for nearly thirty minutes eating slowly and pondering what her next course of action should be, eventually deciding that she should leave before the staff got concerned. *My description will be everywhere before long. It won't be much to go off of, but it will be something.*

I need to get some different clothes.

Morgan's legs were starting to feel hollow from the amount of walking she had done, but finally, she entered a small thrift shop with a suit, some T-shirts, and a sundress displayed in the window.

She lifted her hood and started scanning the large room for clothes that could look like they came from her old wardrobe. She picked up a pink sweatshirt with some college she had never heard of on it, a pair of muddy white snow boots, and a long, denim skirt with a few light stains. She took them into a dressing room, finding the skirt uncomfortably squeezed her waist, the sweatshirt was definitely too big, and the shoes were tight. Nothing was going to fall off or cut off her circulation, so she would have to deal with it.

She hurried to the counter and paid without making eye contact with the cashier. Morgan didn't have to worry about acting normal around her since she was looking at her phone the whole time. Once she'd changed into her new clothes in the dressing rooms, she hurried to the back door she had spotted earlier, shielded from the cashier's gaze by the clothing racks.

Outside the back of the store, there were a few boxes full of clothes wrapped in plastic, some trash bags, and a dumpster. Morgan carefully untied one of the trash bags, pushing some of the clothes aside so that she could slide her own bloodstained ones into the middle of the bag. She sat her old shoes on top, re-tied the bag, and tossed it into the dumpster. Before walking away, she found a sewer grate and tossed the knife and pen into the darkness.

A tightening sensation immediately returned to her legs when she started walking again, and a dull ache still throbbed in her cheek. The buildings gradually got shorter as she walked out of the business area and toward the suburbs. Eventually, she sat down on the curb, taking off her bag and sitting it next to her before wiping her running nose with the inside of her shirt.

People walked by, some of their looks lingering on the frail, red-nosed child sitting by the road.

None said a word.

Morgan wrapped the baggy sweatshirt tightly around herself as the wind started to creep in through her sleeves.

The sun wasn't far from dipping below the tall buildings in the distance, when Morgan was snapped out of her daze by a voice.

"Hello? Excuse me!" the voice said. Morgan turned to see a man in a police uniform with a patchy mustache.

"Are you lost?" he asked. Morgan didn't answer.

"Where are your parents?" he tried again. Morgan's vision blurred with tears. She had wanted to break down crying for a while now, but after she heard those words, she couldn't hold it in anymore. "If you tell me your parents' phone number, I can call them and tell them to come get you," the man offered.

"No," Morgan said quietly with a sniff. "I don't know what happened... There was screaming and blood," she said in a partial lie. A perfectly timed tear rolled down her face.

"I'll take you down to the station. It's going to be okay," he said, offering Morgan his hand to help her up. "What's your name?" he asked, taking out his radio.

"Morgan Toner," she answered.

Holding a packet of tissues in her lap, Morgan

rode in the backseat of the squad car, her bag beside her. The tears wouldn't stop. No matter how she felt, whether it was anger, sadness, relief, or fear, they continued to flow.

Morgan reached for the medical tape on her face, and peeled it away, revealing the red gash covered with partially dried blood, along with some fresh blood starting to fall down her chin. The tears burned her face as they flowed into the opening.

The officer glanced back in the rear view mirror. His eyes widened.

"Oh my — Um, I think we should take you to the hospital for that."

"I don't have enough money to pay for it," said Morgan, "and I don't know anyone that would pay to get it fixed."

"Don't worry, it'll be taken care of," said the officer, making a U-turn at the first opportunity.

"Okay," Morgan said quietly.

Morgan was taken into the ER, and after waiting a while, she was taken to a room where the nurses informed her that her injury would require more than some iodine and a bandaid.

When Morgan walked out, she had stitches across her cheek. She continued to remind herself that it wasn't a good idea to keep running her fingers across it while she was escorted back into the police car to be taken to the station.

The police led her into a cold interview room and offered her a chair on one side of the table, facing the large mirror that was on the wall. Morgan sat down, fidgeting with the zipper of her coat.

Before long, a man entered the room. His face was frozen in an intense expression, with his straw-colored brows dipping low into his eyes and his mouth pressed into a thin line.

"Hello Morgan, I'm Detective Stacey. I'm here to ask you some questions. Before we start, I have some very bad news. I understand if you will want to wait a little while before answering the questions."

"What is it?" Morgan asked, expecting the news of her parents' death.

"Your parents have passed away. They were killed last night by an unknown person. I'm sorry for your loss," he said gravely.

Morgan felt a twinge of anger at her parents and at the police. *Sorry? If they knew what they did… But, killing them was a bad idea, wasn't it?* Morgan shuddered a breath, tears beginning to fall for what seemed like the hundredth time that day.

"Do you need a few minutes?" asked the detective.

"A few," she said, voice barely above a whisper.

"I'll come back in a couple of minutes. Let me know if you need more time."

Morgan sniffled as she nodded. The detective left the room.

Morgan buried her head in her hands as her tears,

and nagging thoughts in her head returned at full force. *Am I worse than them?*

After making sure she would be able to hold back her tears, she lifted her head. She stared into her reflection on the two-way mirror, and in looking at the disgraced girl she saw reflected back at her, she wished the glass would shatter.

Detective Stacey came back in moments later.

"Are you ready, or do you need a little more time?"

"I'm ready."

"Okay. Just let me know if you need a break."

"Okay." Morgan nodded.

"Did your parents ever do anything like leave doors unlocked some nights or anything that would allow someone to get in?" Stacey began, his voice losing its softened edge.

"They would usually leave it unlocked when one of them was home."

"And you were home yesterday night, right?"

"Yes."

"Did you see or hear anything suspicious?"

"I heard my father yelling and my mom screaming for a little bit, but it went really quiet after a few minutes. I thought something bad had happened, like maybe they were fighting or someone broke in." Morgan focused on keeping her voice somber and her breathing steady. "I thought about jumping out the window, but it was too far down, so I grabbed my backpack so I could throw something if there was someone down there. I ran downstairs to their bedroom, but my parents had blood all over them and they weren't moving. Then, a man ran out of the corner and swung at me with a knife," she said, gesturing to the cut on her face. "Then I ran out the back door."

"Do you remember what the man looked like?"

"Not really. He was wearing a ski mask and a dark hoodie I think? His skin in the eye holes looked kind of gray in the lighting, but I couldn't see anything else. I'm sorry." Morgan cast her gaze down to her lap.

"You don't need to be sorry. Any information you can give us will be helpful in finding who did this. Did he grab you or anything? We might be able to find some evidence on your clothes or backpack."

"He didn't touch me except for this." She touched the stitches on her face.

"Okay." He sighed, running a hand through his hair, but quickly put on a smile. "You did a great job. All of this is going to help us a lot."

Morgan was then sent to emergency foster care. Although living there was better than with her parents, the family she was put with had neither the time nor the resources to properly care for her. During her time there, she received call after call from the police, giving her updates, asking for more details on her relationship with her parents, asking about their friends and anyone that might want to hurt them. She repeated what she had said in the interview room that day each time, and her parents' case eventually went cold. It wasn't long after that when her time in foster care ended with being cornered in an alleyway and eventually driven off in a police car.

...

Kipp let out the breath she was holding in. "So you didn't do anything to Grace."

"I was going to. I was about to. I was standing in her closet with a *knife.* The idea that I even thought about it is awful..." Morgan shivered as a cold breeze went by.

"You had a right to be angry at that girl. Not a right to kill her, but guess what? You didn't. And your parents? Your entire life could have been ruined if you stayed under their thumb. And that guy that tried to assault you? He kind of had it coming."

"What are you *saying?* You know about my parents, and now, Grace. You're doing all this investigation work, and helping out the police department, and you haven't told anyone that I'm pretty much a serial killer. Why don't you just turn me in already?"

"Because I love you!" Kipp immediately reeled back. She hadn't meant to say it. She shouldn't have said it.

Morgan's posture straightened as she breathed in. She looked all the way up at Kipp at that point, no longer staring through her lashes. She swallowed, attempting to come up with something to say.

"I didn't think you actually liked me that much," she said finally, her voice so soft that it barely drifted to Kipp's ears.

"Well, I definitely do. What about you? Do you like me?" Kipp's heart drooped as she took in the shock on Morgan's face.

"Yeah. Yes, I do. I just didn't— I *don't* want you to have to deal with me," Morgan sputtered out.

Kipp scoffed, relief pulling a smile onto her face. "Deal with you? Clearly you're pretty considerate, you know, since you'd rather try to force your feelings to disappear than risk bothering me. I'd be more than glad to 'deal' with you."

Morgan didn't reply. She only stared into Kipp's eyes, lips slightly parted. She looked to be contemplating the words that still hung in the air.

Her brow furrowed a bit. "You... You said you loved me. That was the first time anyone has said 'I love you' to me."

"If you want to be my girlfriend, I could tell you that all the time." Kipp's heart nearly skipped a beat as Morgan's eyes became red-rimmed. Kipp wondered if she was about to have some kind of breakdown.

That question was answered as Morgan took a step forward and wrapped her arms tightly around Kipp's waist, resting her head under Kipp's chin.

Breathing in the vanilla scent of Morgan's hair, Kipp smiled as wide as the muscles in her face would allow. "Do you want to come over to my house for dinner tomorrow?" Kipp asked, their bodies still pressed flush against each other. Morgan pulled away, looking up at Kipp with a smile.

"I'd love to," she said.

As Kipp walked Morgan back to Detective Carson's house, she extended her hand. A beat passed before Morgan saw the gesture and placed her hand over Kipp's. Their fingers intertwined, immediately making Morgan's smile grow.

"Are you blushing?" Kipp asked with a teasing smile. Morgan lifted a hand to her face.

"I guess?" she said with a laugh.

When they got to Detective Carson's porch, Morgan turned around at the door, quickly leaning into another hug. Kipp felt her smile against her neck. When they pulled away, they looked at each other for a moment, and Kipp wondered if she should lean forward for a kiss.

Morgan spoke before she could do anything else. "I'll see you tomorrow."

Chapter 11

The smell of coffee and sugar was fresh in the air as Kipp walked in with Morgan, leading her by the hand to a table where Nikki, Isabel, and Luke were waiting. Jackets and sweaters hung off of all of their chairs. Isabel was the first to stick out her hand to Morgan for a hand shake. Nikki didn't move a muscle. Kipp tried to catch her eye, but Nikki never looked over at her.

"I'm Isabel, nice to meet you."

"Hi, I'm Morgan," she said with a smile as she shook Isabel's hand.

"I'm Luke." Luke waved cheerily, tucking away his sketchbook. Morgan waved back. Her eyes then shifted to the person who had yet to introduce herself. Nikki simply tipped her head up.

"Nikki," she said with a smile that never made it to her eyes. Morgan nodded, letting out an anxious breath. Kipp pulled out two chairs for them both, gesturing for Morgan to sit down.

"How long have you guys been together?" asked Isabel. Morgan looked to Kipp.

"Not very long," Kipp said as she plopped down in the chair. "Like, three days counting this one."

"Oh, wow, so this is pretty new!" said Isabel.

"Where did you guys meet?" Luke asked, swatting some hair away from his eyes.

"She's staying with a detective that I've talked to before, Amelia Carson. We met when I was working with Carson on the Anthony Hall stuff."

Luke perked up at that, a thought apparently popping into his head.

"Oh! Did Kipp tell you that she talked to a murderer? Like, a really young one, when she was looking into the Hall drug case?"

Kipp stiffened, picking up on how Morgan's eyes widened.

"Uh, yeah, she— She did," Morgan replied.

"That was crazy!" Luke exclaimed.

"Yep." Nikki raised her brows, eyes fixed on Morgan.

"Do you know any more about that drug ring case?" Luke asked.

Kipp smiled in relief that the subject was shifting. "Yeah, there was this guy trying to get drugs out of a storage locker. They were all stuffed in an old couch." She relaxed a little more seeing Morgan stop fidgeting with her shirt and scratching at her neck.

As everyone walked back to their cars, Kipp looked over at Nikki as soon as Morgan was far enough behind them, talking to Luke and Isabel. Nikki noticed Kipp's eyes boring holes into the side of her head.

"What?" Nikki squinted.

"You were glaring at her," Kipp said quietly, indicating Morgan with a flick of her eyes.

"I wasn't *glaring*," Nikki retorted.

"Yeah, you kind of were."

"Well, I didn't mean to."

"Do you not like her or something?"

"No, her personality is fine, I'm just worried about you."

"I told you, she's a great person. She's not going to hurt me or anything."

"But how do you *know*?" Nikki pressed. They both quieted as Morgan jogged up to them.

"Amelia is here. I'll see you later," she said.

A smile immediately appeared on Kipp's face and she hugged Morgan goodbye, her face only dropping back into an annoyed expression when Sergeant Carson's car rounded a corner out of sight.

Kipp turned back to Nikki as they continued to walk further into the parking lot.

"I know her better than you do. You said you supported me." Kipp made sure to keep her voice low enough to not alert Isabel and Luke, who were laughing at something on Isabel's phone not twenty feet behind them.

"I support you being happy, but I'm scared she'll try to, you know, *do* something," Nikki said, skating around using any violent words.

"She's not going to do anything! I don't understand why you can't trust me on this."

"Well, excuse me for being concerned that someone capable of cold-blooded murder would try to hurt you."

"Cold-blooded? She was a scared little kid who didn't fully understand her actions!" Kipp whisper-shouted.

A beat of silence passed as Nikki blew a breath of air out of her nose. Kipp couldn't believe Nikki was acting this way about Morgan. When Nikki had worked at the animal shelter in junior year, she would always defend the ones that had attacked people, especially if they were abused. Why couldn't she find it in her to believe Morgan could still be a good person?

By that point Isabel and Luke had caught up to them.

"Guys! Prom is coming up so soon! Well, in like a month, but still. Do we want to meet up at someone's house like we did last year?" asked Isabel.

"Yeah. Do you all want to come to my house?" Luke offered, followed by the rest of the group responding in agreement. Kipp and Nikki both made efforts to smile and ignore the argument they just had.

"Is anyone going with someone?" Isabel asked.

Nikki was the first to perk up. "That guy Cameron from my literature class asked me."

"Nice. He's pretty cute," said Luke. "I don't think I'll go with anyone, because if I was going to bring someone, I'd want it to be special, like, someone I really like."

"Yeah. That makes sense," said Isabel. "I might bring one of my friends that goes to a different school. Not as a date, but just to come hang out with us. One of them was saying she really wanted to come to our prom."

"Are you planning to go with your girlfriend?" Luke asked Kipp.

"I haven't asked her yet," Kipp admitted with a shrug.

"Are you going to do something special, like a sign or something?"

"I don't think I'm gonna do anything crazy. I'll probably just ask her." Kipp said as she pulled out her keys. "See you later!"

Nikki watched as Kipp got in her car and began peeling out of the parking lot. They made eye contact, but neither of them waved or smiled before Kipp turned and drove away. Nikki clenched her jaw as she turned to Luke and Isabel, who were still discussing prom.

"Guys, can we talk for a second?" she asked.

"Yeah, what is it?" asked Luke.

"So, you know that girl from the juvie center that Kipp was talking about a while ago? The one that was in there for murder and was giving info to the police? *That's* her girlfriend."

"Oh." Isabel paused, shooting a glance at Luke, who's freckled face had lost some of its color. She ran a hand through her hair. "Why didn't she tell us?"

"She told me, but when I tried to tell her that this whole thing might not be the best idea, or even when I sounded kind of concerned, she would get really defensive."

"Wait, so was Morgan released?" asked Luke.
"Yeah," said Nikki.

"Maybe she's reformed now. How long was she in jail?" asked Luke.

"I don't know. She must've been arrested when she was pretty young. Kipp keeps telling me that she didn't mean to kill that guy and that she feels bad about it, but I really don't know about that. I'm just worried about it. I found this one article on the case, and apparently Morgan stabbed the guy in the neck with a metal rod."

Luke and Isabel's eyes widened.

Isabel looked a little unnerved, but her voice still came out perfectly calm. "How do you know that wasn't a fake article? They could have just found a random picture of her and wanted to make up some crazy story."

"No, it was definitely real."

"Well, you said she did it when she was really young. I'm sure Morgan wouldn't do something like that again, especially to Kipp."

"And like you said, Kipp said she didn't mean to do it in the first place," said Luke.

"Yeah, but what if Kipp's exaggerating, or lying? If she *really* likes Morgan, she might want to cover for her so we'll leave her alone. Her mom might not even know about Morgan."

"I get where you're coming from with this, but I don't think Kipp would get into a relationship with someone she thought wasn't trustworthy." Luke argued. "Morgan probably went through a lot of trauma and stuff."

Nikki wanted to shake them both by the shoulders. How could they see no issue with this? Kipp could be in serious danger. "But we don't know Morgan well. Maybe Kipp is missing some red flags because she's so enamored or something," Nikki countered.
"I think you need to relax," said Luke "Morgan seemed like a nice person. I got a good vibe from her. She really doesn't seem like the type to manipulate someone into a relationship to hurt them."

"You can't just go off of a *vibe!* What if she gets triggered somehow and she tries to attack Kipp?" Nikki questioned.

"I think Kipp would be able to handle that," said Isabel. "If Morgan is the same person as that girl at the facility, then I agree it's a little weird that Kipp didn't say something. But I think we need to give her the benefit of the doubt. She was probably afraid of all of us being super worried for her and trying to break her and Morgan up. This whole thing makes me a little worried too, but I think we should give Morgan a chance and get to know her more first."

"I think I'm going to talk to Kipp. Like, try to get her to describe the relationship to make sure there aren't any bad signs that she's not noticing," said Nikki.

Luke and Isabel exchanged uneasy looks. "If you think that's a good idea," said Luke.

Nikki split off from Isabel and Luke and made a beeline for her car.

Within ten minutes, she was knocking on Kipp's door. She had gone over what she was going to say over and over again in the car.

"Hey," Kipp said flatly as she opened the door. "What brings you here?"

"I didn't like how that cafe thing ended and I wanted to ask if you wanted to go on a walk. Like, maybe on the trails you like to run on behind your house?"

"Is this so you can have a heart to heart with me about how much of a monster Morgan is?"

"No, we just haven't had time to catch up in a while. I'm going to give Morgan a chance, and I want us to go back to how things were before. I don't want you to stay mad at me."

Kipp sighed. "I don't want to either."

"Good. Do you want to get going?"

"Sure. The path to the trail is in the back." Kipp closed and locked the door before walking around the side of the house. The backyard was sectioned off from the woods by a tall fence to make sure Milo wouldn't end up running off to get a squirrel. Kipp opened the gate, and they both walked across the uncut grass to a small break in the trees.

A silence settled over Nikki and Kipp as they walked down the tiny trail that eventually connected to the running path. Large roots occasionally stuck out of the ground, threatening to trip anyone not paying attention. Old, soggy leaves carpeted the path, not giving the satisfying crunch that would come from the freshly fallen ones of autumn. The only sounds that could be heard were the cries of the birds and the quiet steps of two friends walking slowly down the trail.

"How's your weekend been?" Kipp asked, splitting the thick silence.

"Good. How's yours?"

"Good. I have some homework to catch up on, though."

"Yeah, me too. Listen, I'm genuinely sorry about the whole Morgan thing. I was just worried. How are you guys doing?" Nikki asked.

"Good," Kipp said with a quick smile. "How are

you and Cameron? Are you going to make it official, or is this just a prom thing?"

"I think we might make it official. We're planning on having a nice dinner the day after prom. Have you gone on a date with Morgan yet?"

"Not yet. She's come over for dinner though."

"What's she like?"

"Uh, shy, I guess? She's sweet."

"Sweet," Nikki repeated. "That's good."

"Are you sure you're not worried about her or…"

"No, no, no. I just wanted to learn a little bit more about her," Nikki assured.

"Okay, just making sure."

Nikki could hear doubt in Kipp's voice, and based on the lack of eye contact her friend was giving her, Nikki assumed Kipp didn't want to talk about it anymore.

The treeline broke in front of a bridge that went over a large creek. Nikki looked to her left to see a flash of blue and white feathers right before it flew off into the sky while Kipp continued onto the bridge. Nikki decided to lighten the mood by pointing out Kipp's favorite bird.

"Look, it's a blue j—"

An agonizingly loud *bang* sounded and rang in her ears. She looked up to see an empty bridge, and a purple bobbing sweatshirt in the water below.

Chapter 12

"Kipp!" Nikki screamed, her voice muffled by the ringing in her ears. She looked back as a barely visible figure in the far distance of the woods took off running. What was *happening?*

Nikki ran off the path, pushed past the trees, and went down the slope to the river bank. She waded into the icy water as Kipp groaned and turned to float on her back. She was alive.

It took a second for Kipp to break out of the shock of what had just happened. It was a strange sensation to feel as if you are going unbelievably fast, and at the same time stuck in slow motion, with no escape from either. Fragments of memories began to enter Kipp's mind as familiar adrenaline started pumping through her. Suddenly, she was back in the car. She squeezed her eyes shut as the windshield shattered and the car swerved and rolled off the road. Her hearing left her, saving her ears from the horrible screeching and crunching of metal and glass. She opened her eyes, hanging upside down with agony in her ribs. Tears started to fall, coating her lashes with salty liquid that was quick to turn cold. She covered her eyes at the sight of her parents' limp bodies hanging by their seatbelts in the front seats. Her arms began to ache, but she kept her hands clamped over her eyes. The memory faded as she started to hear splashing

The cold water pulled her back to the present as she felt a hand grab her arm. She opened her eyes and took a deep breath.

"Not dead," Kipp announced as Nikki tried to pull her out of the river. "I got it, it's okay," Kipp insisted as she stood up on the river bank, her clothes clinging to her skin.

"You don't look okay," Nikki said. Kipp hissed as she removed her hand from her shoulder to reveal a bloody streak.

"It's fine, I can barely feel it. Let's just get back to my house." Kipp attempted a smile.

Nikki grimaced. "Do you need to go to the hospital or something?"

"I think I can handle it since there's no bullet to be taken out. It's basically a bad scratch," said Kipp.

The two walked back to her house, the ringing slowly fading out of both of their ears, but the cold water still chilled Kipp to the bone. She felt miserable. It almost reminded her of how she'd felt right after the car crash. She remembered sitting on the edge of a clean white hospital bed with her feet dangling off as she took in deep breaths, her ribs throbbing with pain. She'd gritted her teeth, pursed her lips, anything that might help her refrain from shedding tears. She had to be strong. Just like she had to be strong now.

"That was… insane," said Nikki. "I mean, someone shot at you! And they could've shot me too!"

"Yeah, that was crazy." Kipp focused on the path in front of them to keep her steady against the weightlessness she was feeling.

"Why would someone do that?"

"It might've been a hunter that accidentally came into the area."

"That would be some accident. You think someone wandered so far from designated grounds that they made it over to a running trail and shot at a person they thought was a deer?"

"I guess. What else would it be?"

"I don't know. Something to do with that drug case maybe."

"Why would they come after me?"

"Well, I don't know how involved you are."

Kipp looked down at her feet. "Not enough to have Hall send someone after me. It was probably a hunter that didn't want to get in trouble for almost shooting someone so they ended up running away."

Kipp clenched her fists at how disingenuous her voice sounded. It would be clear to almost anyone that even she didn't believe it. She looked up to see that Nikki's expression had relaxed a bit.

When the two entered the house, Kipp immediately ducked into the laundry room. She pulled down the side of the shirt by the shoulder. The graze looked worse than it felt, but some of the blood was already clotting, sticky and dark. She hadn't lied to Nikki. It *was* basically a bad scratch.

She slapped a large Band-Aid over her wound. Then, she pulled out some random clothing from the dryer and changed into them, but not before wringing her hair out onto her already soaked clothes. Kipp had just thrown the dripping clothes in the washer when she heard her mother's voice.

"How was the walk?" Roberta asked, but her expression scrunched up in confusion as she saw that Kipp had changed into a mismatched outfit and her hair was wet with some of the water soaking into the longsleeve shirt by her shoulders. "What happened?" Roberta asked. Nikki turned to Kipp, who hesitated, but mostly made up for it with a quick partial truth,

"I fell into the river," she said with a forced laugh. Roberta laughed in return.

"Oh no! I'm guessing you didn't fall in though?" She turned to Nikki, who let out a nervous chuckle.

"No," she said.

"That's good. You didn't hurt yourself, did you?"

Roberta asked, directing her attention back to Kipp.

"Nope," Kipp answered, seeing Nikki's concerned expression out of the corner of her eye. "We're gonna go up to my room. I put my wet clothes in the washer." Kipp slowly moved toward the stairwell, hoping Nikki would take the hint and follow her. Nikki flashed a smile at Roberta before hurrying over to the stairs.

"You should probably put some disinfectant on that. Do you have Neosporin or something?" Nikki said as soon as Kipp's door was shut.

"Yeah, it's probably down here." Kipp rifled through the disorganized cabinet under the sink before pulling out a yellow tube of cream.

"Wasn't Morgan getting notes from Hall?"

Nikki's question went unanswered as Kipp pretended to be too focused on tending to her wound. "Kipp," Nikki said louder.

"Hm?"

"Didn't Morgan get notes from Anthony Hall?"

"We don't know that for sure. There's no way to prove it."

"But it wasn't disproven."

"No, but—"

"Kipp, you have to at least acknowledge that being around Morgan is dangerous at this point."

Kipp forcefully pressed the bandaid back on her arm. "I thought you said you were done talking about Morgan."

"I said I'd give her a chance, but you almost getting shot because of her doesn't have anything to do with her personality and me liking her or not. This is actually a really dangerous situation."

"How do you know that wasn't just a hunter out there?"

Nikki stepped forward. "There is a tiny fraction of a chance that it is. Do you know how many things would have to happen for a hunter to end up all the way over here shooting at people?"

"It could happen. And it could also just be some random crazy person."

Nikki groaned. "I'm not telling you to break up with Morgan, I'm just saying you should probably stay away from her for a while. She'd probably understand if you said, 'Hey, I don't want to get shot, so can we take a break?'"

"No." Kipp turned around to look Nikki dead in the eye. "It already took a lot of effort to get her to see that I like her and that she deserved me. If I suddenly say that it's her fault I got shot at, she might never talk to me again."

"Okay, then just try not to go out with her." Nikki's voice was becoming high pitched and pleading. "You can call her and stuff, but just don't go places where you'll be seen with her."

"She's not stupid. She'll know something is up, and then she'll think I'm embarrassed of her or something. And if this is Hall, which is a pretty big if, how do you know Morgan is the reason he's after me?" Kipp crossed her arms.

"Of course she is!" Nikki said. "You're not involved in the case, and she is! She's getting all these notes from him, and—"

"I am involved in the case!" Kipp burst out. "I saw one of Hall's drug deals in an abandoned house a few months ago, and last week on a patrol, I got one of his dealers arrested! He knows who I am. I'm not letting him wreck my relationship."

Nikki's mouth closed. She stared at Kipp as if she couldn't believe what she was hearing. Then, she said, "And you didn't tell me? Or Luke or Isabel?"

Kipp didn't say anything.

Nikki snatched her jacket off the bed and started toward the door.

"Fine. Do whatever you want." The door slammed behind her.

The next morning, Kipp's eyes opened to Milo licking her face. She buried her head underneath her pillow, waving for him to leave. Instead, he jumped on the bed and lay next to her. She rolled onto her side, immediately regretting it when her wound throbbed. Hunger began scratching at her stomach, eventually luring her to groggily roll out of bed.

The Sunday morning light had fully illuminated the house, and her mother had already left for work. Kipp placed two pieces of toast into the toaster, and waited with a plate and a jar of jelly. Milo bounded into the kitchen, impatiently waiting for Kipp to feed him. She had no energy after last night. That was the first time she and Nikki had ever had a real fight. Why should she have told her about Hall?

After Kipp finished her breakfast and fed Milo, she decided she'd go for a walk. She grabbed an athletic shirt, jacket, and leggings, along with her running shoes. Clipping on Milo's harness and leash, she set off into the woods, walking along the same path she had taken with Nikki yesterday.

Walking in solitude, with only her dog, and the singing birds was usually comforting to Kipp. But right now, it only felt dangerously isolated.

A twig snapped.

Kipp whipped her head around, trying to find the source of the sound, but there was nothing there. Focusing on her rapidly quickening breaths, Kipp ignored the shadows in her peripheral vision that seemed to form human-like shapes. She heard a small crunch of leaves, and her stomach immediately burned with fear. Kipp frantically looked around, scanning the forest floor, and the branches above. Her eyes finally landed on a squirrel scampering up a tree.

She sighed in relief, although her palms were still damp. Kipp managed to push down her thoughts of hearing gunshots, and falling down dead on the lonely trail, her friends and mother wondering where she was. It would probably take days to find her body if she was murdered here. Kipp shook the thoughts from her head and pushed onward.

She and Milo finally reached their usual stopping point, and the two turned around and began to walk back to the safety of home. Again, she heard a small sound behind her. Kipp refused to give into her urge to whip around, and instead forced herself to continue walking, quickening her pace.

Kipp's anxiety grew with every step, like a balloon in her chest that was close to popping. She pursed her lips. She walked faster, faster, and faster still. Finally, the balloon burst, and she broke out into a run, stealing glances behind her. Milo happily ran beside her, unaware of the fear swirling inside Kipp's head. The brave Kipp Green, running from nothing, and everything.

What if that was Hall? she thought. She had *seen* things related to the case. She had seen Hall himself with a gun in the abandoned building. She'd been with Jordan when they'd found the drugs in the storage locker, too. She was the one that had asked the man from the abandoned building to open it. *Shit.* What if Hall was coming after her?

Kipp arrived at her house, her legs and lungs burning. Three miles. She had run three miles as fast as she could without stopping. Kipp dropped to her knees at the bottom step to her front door, letting her firm hold loosen on Milo's leash, allowing him bound up to the front to wait for it to be opened.

A wave of nausea washed over Kipp. She coughed and dry heaved, thankful she'd chosen to eat a light breakfast that morning. Feeling the nausea quickly retreating, Kipp shakily opened the front door. *What the fuck was that? There was literally nothing there. Why am I acting like a fucking wimp?* Kipp pulled off her jacket and grabbed some of the heaviest weights she owned in an attempt to give her ego time to recover. She pulled them up to her chest over and over again, even as the pain from her shoulder became agonizing. The weights fell to the floor as Kipp lost her grip, sucking in air through her teeth. She glanced at herself in the mirror, her attention drawn to the large bandage peeking out from under her sleeve. A quick sting of pain shot over Kipp's wound as she peeled off the bandage she had put on, and observed the divot. *It's not that bad,* Kipp thought with wobbly confidence.

Kipp's phone started to ring from where she left it on the kitchen counter. It was Nikki.

Kipp was so tired of defending her choices to her. She turned her phone over and let it go to voicemail.

Chapter 13

Kipp licked sweat off her upper lip as she twisted her lacrosse stick in her hands. Her friends watched from the bleachers as the referee motioned for the next play to start.

Morgan was sitting a step down from the group, but she'd made sure to sit sideways so that she would be able to join in on conversation if she was invited. The sun shone down on the field, an occasional cloud bringing momentary shade. The field smelled of freshly cut grass, and pollen could be seen lightly coated on each of the trimmed blades.

Everyone in the almost-full stands clapped as one of Kipp's teammates scored the first point. Morgan was starting to question whether she should have sat next to Kipp's friends.

"Morgan, you're going with Kipp to prom, right?" said Isabel, pulling on a cap with *California Department of Fish and Wildlife* on it.

"I think so." Morgan smiled, glancing to where

Kipp was jogging down the field.

"Oh! Has Kipp told you about the prom committee?" Luke piped up.

"No," Morgan smiled, leaning forward in intrigue.

"Dude, there's two girls in there that *hate* each other. Every meeting they'll get into these really passive-aggressive arguments and one time one of them got detention because she threw a pencil at the other and it hit her in the eye. I really wish I was on the committee now. I'd bring popcorn every time."

Morgan let out a small laugh. "I would too. It sounds entertaining."

She felt unbelievably content sitting there and watching her girlfriend play. Kipp's friends were so nice. Morgan never felt the need to fidget or wrap her arms around herself, she just sat there smiling. Her only concern was Nikki. She didn't seem to like her very much at the cafe. Maybe she was just having a rough day, but Morgan couldn't help but feel like Nikki disapproved of her. Kipp said no one knew about her conviction, so it couldn't be that. Maybe she just needed to get to know her more.

"What have you been up to the past few days?" Morgan asked Nikki.

"The past few days?" Nikki paused. "I... went on a walk with Kipp?" She said it with a confused expression, as if she expected Morgan to have known that already.

"That sounds nice. Where did you go?"

"In the woods behind her house." Nikki glanced at the lacrosse field, pursing her lips. Morgan considered that there was something Nikki wasn't telling her. *Did Nikki tell Kipp she didn't like me? Or is it something that doesn't involve me at all?*

Morgan's attention was pulled back to the field as another round of claps and cheers started up as Kipp ran toward the goal. When she was just ten feet away, she shot. The ball whizzed past the goal, missing it by a few inches. Kipp grabbed her arm, hunching over as she scowled at her shoulder. Morgan glanced behind her. Nikki's eyes were locked on the field as she rubbed her temples, mouth fixed in a frown. Morgan looked back at Kipp. Did she get hurt?

"What happened?" Luke questioned. "Kipp barely ever misses a shot, and that was literally right next to the goal. It looked like her arm was bothering her."

"Maybe she pulled a muscle?" Isabel offered as she watched Kipp continue playing after waving off a concerned teammate. "She looks okay though."

"Mhm," Nikki grunted.

After the game, Kipp invited Morgan over to her house to watch a movie. Hopefully it would take her mind off of all the mistakes she'd made during the game. She'd been planning all day to ask Morgan to prom. Though it was one simple collection of words, Kipp repeated it in her head over and over again, practicing and perfecting the line. It was only a few weeks before prom. Kipp invited Morgan over to her house with the sole purpose of asking that simple question. They were sitting on the old, brown leather couch with squishy cushions, watching an action comedy that had recently been released.

"Do you want to go to prom with me?" Kipp said finally. "It's in about three weeks and I've already bought tickets, so you don't have to pay for yours."

Conflicted emotions flickered across Morgan's face. "I'd love to. Is there a dress code? Or a theme we have to follow?"

"People are strongly encouraged to wear formal stuff, but there's no rule against not. There's also a theme, but no one has to dress for it. You definitely don't have to wear a dress if you don't want to."

"I do *want* to wear a dress. One that's not like the ones I wore when I was with my parents, but I feel like it would still make me feel icky." Morgan folded her arms. "That sounds kind of contradictory. What I mean is that I would want to wear a dress, as in I like the concept of it, but I'm scared if I do find one that I like, I will feel weird actually wearing it even if I love how it looks."

"That's totally fine! There's plenty of non-dress options. I mean, I'm probably going to end up wearing a suit."

"I'm not really a suit kind of person, but I'm sure I'll figure something out."

The two were sitting inches apart, hands

intertwined. Kipp considered putting her arm around Morgan, but the thought of making her uncomfortable kept her still. More and more of her attention focused on the fact that Morgan's arm was barely brushing hers. Finally, she asked,

"Hey, are you okay if I put my arm around you?" she asked during a relatively boring scene.

"Oh, sure. Yeah, that's fine."

"Okay." Kipp pulled her hand away from Morgan's, allowing her to lift her arm and drape it over her girlfriend's shoulders. She bit the inside of her cheek as her hurt shoulder screamed for her to put her arm down. Apparently the labored breath she let out wasn't quiet enough.

"Is everything okay?" Morgan asked.

"Yeah, my shoulder is just really sore from the game."

"Oh. Do you want something for it? I don't really know what would help, but we might have something."

"It's fine. Soreness usually goes away after a few days." Kipp hated seeing Morgan worry. She couldn't even imagine what kind of reaction she would have if Kipp told her she had been shot at. Knowing Morgan, she would probably blame herself no matter what Kipp said. There was no way Kipp was going to cause her more grief.

The sun was just starting to brush the tops of the

trees when Amelia picked Morgan up.

"Did you have fun?" the sergeant asked as Morgan opened the car door.

"Yes."

"What did you guys do?"

"We watched a movie and talked a little about prom."

"Did Kipp ask you to prom?"

"Yes." Morgan tried to make sure her smile wasn't too wide. "It's three weeks from now."

"She could've said something a little sooner," Amelia said with an exasperated laugh. "I'm very busy the next few weeks, but I promise I'll find a time to go with you to find a dress. Remind me later and we can look for some stores."

The car stopped in front of Amelia's home, where both of them got out and headed up the steps. They could see something on the doormat: a stray piece of mail, a plain white envelope left in the very center of the mat. Morgan stopped to pick it up. She stepped back so Amelia could open the door as she looked at it.

She turned it over to look at the other side, and what had originally been a twinge of unease turned into bone-crushing dread. There was no stamp, no address, nothing but her name written in cheap black marker on the front.

She whipped around to look up and down the street. Nothing looked out of the ordinary. No strange cars, no people other than a couple walking their dog. Morgan felt like dozens of eyes were boring holes through her even as she turned to walk inside.

"Amelia," she called, dropping the letter on a table as if it was on fire.

"What?" Amelia closed the door and walked over.

"There's another one."

"Oh," Amelia breathed as she noticed the letter.

"I touched it." Morgan curled her hands into fists. "Now my fingerprints are going to be all over it. They won't think I made it, will they?"

"No. You did nothing wrong. Let's take it down to the precinct and we can open it there." Amelia grabbed a nearby pair of mittens and put one on to move the letter into a Ziploc bag.

They drove down to the precinct with Morgan holding the bagged letter. When they got there, they went straight to the captain's office.

"We've got a development in the Hall case," Amelia said, lifting the bag in the air. The captain immediately got up from his desk as Amelia set the bag down. "I'm going to go get some gloves and an evidence bag." She jogged off.

"Where did you guys find this?" asked Brumbly.

"It was on the doorstep," said Morgan. "I picked it up and Amelia put it in a bag with some mittens. There was no one around when we found it."

"Are there security cameras by your door? Or one

of those doorbells with the cameras?"

"No. There's one that faces the sidewalk, but not one that completely shows the porch. You could avoid the one that shows the sidewalk pretty easily if you wanted to."

"Ah, well, we can check that later. Maybe whoever left it slipped up."

Amelia came back into the office with a slightly larger bag and a pair of latex gloves.

"Do you want to open this here or in the evidence room?" the sergeant asked.

"Here is fine."

Amelia nodded once before she pulled on the gloves and opened the bag.

"What if there's something bad in it?" Morgan said quickly as Amelia grabbed a pen to slide under the sealed flap.

"I don't think Hall has access to any bioweapons, and this surely isn't big enough for a bomb, so I think we'll be okay. You can step out if you want," said Amelia. Morgan stayed still for a second before backing away to stand near the door. Amelia carefully opened the letter with a pen, pulling out a sheet of folded up paper.

"Can you read it to me? I left my reading glasses at home today," said the captain.

"It's up to Morgan. Do you want to hear?" Amelia looked at Morgan, who tipped her chin up and nodded.

"Okay, then I'll read it. 'Looks like you're finally out. I'm sure Daniel's family is ecstatic about it. I can't wait to say hello to you in person. I hope you still like solving mysteries, because I have another one for you.' Under that there's what looks like a cipher. Are you doing okay, Morgan? You look a little pale."

"I'm fine," Morgan replied. Of course Hall would bring up one of the worst days of her life. "I don't understand how he's still monitoring me! I haven't done any research on your computer, and I'm not in the training school anymore."

"We'll figure it out," Amelia assured.

The captain took the note from the sergeant. "I can take this to get some pictures of it and try to lift some prints. We can work on figuring out the code after that."

Thirty miles away, Kipp, Nikki, Isabel, and Luke were in Denver, shopping for prom. The formalwear outlet looked unassuming with its red brick walls and a tin roof. Inside, it was filled with rows and rows of dresses in plastic covers. As the group looked around, Kipp folded her arms, examining the different dresses on display. She picked up a few in her size from the racks, deciding she'd give some dresses a shot before fully committing to a suit.

"Guys," Isabel called from inside her room. "Everyone should come out of the dressing rooms at the same time and show what they picked out until we all find one we really like! It'll be like a mini fashion show."

"Yeah, we should count down," said Luke. "Okay, three, two, one!"

Each person stepped out of their dressing room. Nikki's dress was a plain, dark purple mermaid-style dress, Isabel had picked out a light pink gown with small flowers on it, and Luke had found a suit with a flamingo pattern.

"That's a great dress, Kipp," Nikki laughed. "I have to ask what your thought process was when you decided on that one."

"Yeah…" Kipp began, looking down at the admittedly hideous bright orange dress she had on. "I honestly don't know. I just kind of thought, 'Oh yeah, orange is my favorite color so, you know,' and it didn't come out well." She huffed out a laugh as she moved to slip back into the dressing room.

"What happened?" Isabel asked.

Kipp turned back around. Isabel was pointing to her shoulder. "I fell into the river by my house and a rock scratched me."

"How did you manage to just fall into the river?" Luke laughed.

"My bike went over a rock, and I fell off the bridge," Kipp said quietly. Isabel looked alarmed, and Luke opened his mouth, but Kipp didn't want to have to lie to them again. She flashed a smile before walking back into the dressing room.

She started pulling off the dress, glancing at her exposed bandaid. It definitely didn't feel good to lie to her friends, but it was better this way. The more they knew, the more danger they'd be in. She put the orange dress back in its bag and tried on another, this one a more tight-fitting red dress. When she stepped out and looked in the mirror, it definitely looked better than the orange one, although it still wasn't what she was looking for, not to mention the fabric on the inside was scratchy despite the velvety outside.

Just as she had pulled her regular clothes back on, there was a knock on the wall of the dressing room. Kipp pulled the curtain back to see Nikki on the other side.

"You haven't told Isabel and Luke about the thing?" Nikki whispered, leaning forward.

"The thing?"

"The walk."

"No. I thought you wanted me to 'do whatever I want,'" Kipp said with air quotes.

Nikki rolled her eyes. "I was frustrated. I'm sorry if I hit a nerve about Morgan, but I want you to realize how scary this situation is. I feel like Luke and Isabel should know about it."

"I'll tell them later. I promise," said Kipp. Nikki went back to her dressing room. This was slowly turning into torture. Not only was she still lying to everyone around her, but she'd roped Nikki into it, too. But, she couldn't afford to pull more people into the Hall situation.

A while later, they had all come out of the rooms, except for Luke.

"Hey guys, I think this is the one," Luke announced as he stepped out, striking a pose in a glittery purple blazer.

"Nice. I like that one. Are you actually going to wear it?" asked Kipp.

"Yeah. I mean, it's senior prom. Might as well wear something flashy."

"I keep forgetting that this'll be the last prom we'll ever go to," Isabel said as she held a fluffy peach dress in her arms.

"Yeah," Nikki agreed, "when I was trying to decide between my top two dresses, for a second I was like, 'Oh I can just wear the other next year.'" She turned to where Kipp was standing empty-handed. A moment of silence passed before Nikki said with a strained smile, "Kipp, did you find a dress?"

"No. I was thinking about it, but I think I'll wear a tux. It'll be fun to switch it up a little. Then I can wear some matching dress shoes and not kill my feet with a pair of heels like I did for junior prom." She couldn't get herself to meet Nikki's eyes as she talked. "It's really weird to think it's been four years since our first dance. Well, mine and Nikki's anyway. You guys had middle school dances." Kipp gestured to Isabel and Luke.

"Well, they weren't really dances since no one danced," said Luke. "We would just kind of stand there awkwardly while some of the teachers danced because they thought that would encourage us. The only fun part was talking with friends about all the drama floating around. It was mainly just classic middle school drama. You know, like, 'Oh did you hear so-and-so asked so-and-so to the dance and got rejected.'"

"Middle school drama is ridiculous," said Nikki. "Some people would get so offended over nothing. Like, there were these two kids that 'dated' for I think three days, and they broke up because the girl was mad that the guy didn't let her take his sweatshirt home."

"Oh my God, I remember that!" Kipp exclaimed with a laugh, finally meeting Nikki's eyes. "I really wish we all knew each other in middle school. That would've been so much fun."

"Yeah. But at least we found each other here," said Isabel.

"I think we have you to thank for that," said Kipp, "since you were the one that invited me and Nikki to sit with you guys." The air around them seemed so much less tense. She hoped Nikki would let them go back to normal and forget all the stress their relationship had been put under.

Each of them, save for Kipp, walked out with a

bag containing the clothes they would be wearing to their final prom. Nikki stuck with the purple dress, Isabel was almost skipping with her peach-colored one, and Luke was glowing with excitement about his purple sequin suit.

They all got in Isabel's car to go home. Kipp sat next to Nikki in the backseat, trying her best to not make it awkward. Nikki never even returned a smile. As Isabel and Luke talked about prom and joked about exchanging corsages with each other, Nikki kept glancing at Kipp, as if she expected her to blurt out right there that she had lied to them. Kipp felt like she was digging herself a bigger hole with every person she didn't tell.

When school was let out for the day, Luke invited the group to his house for homework. They all settled in Luke's kitchen. While Luke went to wash graphite off the side of his hand from the relentless doodling he had done on worksheets that day, Kipp's phone began to ring. She picked up her phone, and upon seeing the captain's profile picture on the screen, immediately pressed the accept button.

"Hello?" the captain said quickly.

"Hey, what's going on?" Kipp asked.

"That man from the storage facility finally cracked. We offered him a deal, and he said Hall will arrive in Rundale by Tuesday."

"What? Holy shit, that's tomorrow!"

"Yeah, we have to move fast. Apparently he has a huge supply of unicorn dust in Rundale that he's going to send off to Utah, which will expand his operation a *lot*. Sergeant Carson and Morgan found a note on their doorstep like the ones Morgan was receiving at the training school. It has a code on it. If you want to come down to the precinct at some point we can show you what we have."

"On my way." Kipp hung up the phone and shoved her homework into her bag. "Sorry guys, something came up with the Anthony Hall thing, I have to go." Kipp threw her backpack over her shoulder and ran to the door.

"Hold on!" she heard Nikki's voice behind her. "I'll walk you out."

"You don't have to. I have to get there fast."

"Then I'll run with you."

Kipp ran to her bike and slammed her helmet on. Nikki darted in front of the bike before Kipp could pedal away.

"What are you *doing?* You can't just go over there."

"Well, that's what I'm doing."

"If you're on Hall's radar, is it really the best idea to go over there right now?"

"Yep," Kipp said, turning the bike so it could weave around Nikki. "Hall isn't going to just waltz into the precinct to get me, and I need to see Morgan. I'll call you later if it makes you feel better."

Nikki was left tugging on her braids as she walked

back inside. She had to fight herself not to run after Kipp.

"How was the run?" Luke laughed when Nikki walked inside. When Nikki didn't smile back, Luke's smile faded. "Did something happen out there?"

"I have something to tell you guys, but you have to promise you won't tell Kipp that I told you."

Isabel looked up from her work. "Are you sure you need to tell us? There might be a good reason why she—"

"No, she's going to get hurt. She already has, which is what I want to tell you."

"Did Morgan do something?" Luke asked quietly, as if Kipp was in the next room.

"No, but she's kind of involved. Me and Kipp went on a walk yesterday and someone shot at us. Kipp's arm got grazed and I don't think she told her mom or anything."

Isabel covered her mouth, and Luke's pen slipped out of his hand.

Nikki continued. "Morgan was getting these threats from that drug ring leader from the case Kipp was learning about. I think they're going after Kipp because she's involved with the case and close with Morgan."

"Why didn't she want to tell us?" asked Isabel.

"I guess she didn't want more people trying to tell her it was a bad idea."

It was silent for a while as Isabel started to pace

and Luke sat with his face frozen in shock.

"So she's going to the precinct right now?" Isabel asked.

"Yeah."

"Maybe we should call her, or go to her house for something like an intervention," said Luke.

"Yeah. I think we need to plan an intervention. We can meet at her house tomorrow morning. I think if we all have the same opinion on stuff, we'll have a better chance of her listening."

"Well, then, let's start planning what we're going to say," Isabel said, pulling out a sheet of paper.

The wind was starting to make Kipp's eyes water as she rode to the precinct. Luke's house was on the outskirts of town, and she had never gone from there to the precinct before. She had pulled up some directions to make sure she didn't get herself lost. She had gotten out of the closely-packed neighborhoods and into a section that looked less maintained. There were a few businesses by the road like an auto parts shop and a nail salon, but they all looked pretty run-down.

"Turn right onto Smith Street," said the navigator. As Kipp turned, her gaze flicked to the street sign, and she nearly ran into a utility pole. Wasn't she just on Franklin Road? Her mind rocketed back to what she had heard in the abandoned building as she stared at the metal warehouse that sat at the intersection of the two roads. *Were they talking about street names instead of people?* There was a small window on the door to the warehouse, and as she passed by, she thought she could see a figure looking at her through it.

Inside the precinct, Kipp was directed to a tidy meeting room with a large circular table made of dark wood and a TV on one of the walls. Everyone was seated at the table. Morgan was surrounded by papers and had a computer in front of her while Sergeant Carson and Captain Brumbly sat across from her.

"Oh, good. You got here pretty fast." The captain got up to greet Kipp.

"Yeah, I might've almost bumped into some people," Kipp admitted. She should have told Brumbly about her theory the second she got there, but something held her back.

A laugh bubbled out of Brumbly. "That's all right. We've been working on this for a while, and it's a pretty complicated code. We gave it out to a lot of the people in the precinct, but Morgan's the only one who's been able to get any progress on it. We can't get any code specialists in until late tomorrow night, or Wednesday, so she's really all we've got."

"How far has she got on it?" Kipp asked as she sat down at the end of the table, pulling over a copy of the code. *If I say something about the warehouse, Hall will try to kill me or Morgan.*

"It has a lot of layers and each one is pretty complicated," Morgan answered, looking up from her scribbling. "It has a different Caesar cipher for each word, and I think the words might spell out numbers. Little code puzzles were my favorite in middle school, so with some online decoders, I think I'll be able to finish tomorrow morning at the latest."

"I like those odds," said Kipp. She noticed a small stuffed bear in Morgan's lap. "What's that?"

"Oh," Amelia laughed, "Davey brought it for Morgan after I told him about you two."

Kipp chuckled, looking to Morgan. "I didn't know you liked stuffed animals."

"They're comforting," Morgan said, looking up for a second to smile.

Kipp turned to the captain. "So, what's going to happen tomorrow?"

"We're going to have most of the department out patrolling," said Brumbly, "and we're also going to have some officers from other counties on standby in case things escalate."

"Are there any specific areas you guys are going to have extra surveillance on?"

"We'll put more of an emphasis on areas with a lot of abandoned buildings or storage areas since that's where people connected to Hall have been seen the most."

Kipp nodded. *Okay, so maybe they'll look into the*

warehouse anyway. "Is there any way I can help out? I've barely missed any classes this year, so I can just tell my teachers and my lacrosse coach I won't be there tomorrow."

"About that, could I actually see you in the hallway for a second?"

"Sure." Kipp and Brumbly stepped outside and Brumbly shut the door.

"I know you want to help, so I'm going to give you a job," he said. "Since you won't be in school, I want you to stay in the precinct and make sure Morgan stays safe. Everyone will be very busy, including Sergeant Carson, and there won't be a lot of time to keep an eye on her."

"I could definitely do that, but are you sure you won't need help with patrolling or anything?"

"Morgan's well-being could depend on you if something happens, so I'd really like for you to stay back. Can you do that?"

"Yeah."

"Great. Try to be here by nine tomorrow morning." Brumbly opened the door and they both walked back into the room. The captain sat down next to Sergeant Carson and they began looking over some files.

Kipp spent a few minutes looking over Morgan's shoulder even though she didn't really understand anything that Morgan had written on the different pieces of paper. Her mind drifted to tomorrow.

Since she'd be looking after Morgan, and they'd both be safe in the precinct, she could tell Brumbly about the warehouse with no worries. *But what if Hall finds out tonight somehow? I'll just play it safe and tell them tomorrow. If they are hiding drugs or criminals there, hopefully they won't be gone by tomorrow. I really should tell* someone, *though. Maybe I can wait until me and Morgan are alone and tell her.*

Kipp sat down a seat away from Morgan since the slew of papers extended to each neighboring seat. After a while of discussing plans for tomorrow with Amelia, Captain Brumbly excused himself to go home. Soon after, Amelia left to get her and Morgan some dinner.

Cheek resting on her hand, Kipp watched as Morgan worked. She couldn't help but smile while Morgan remained in her own little world of letters, numbers, and logic. Morgan never ceased to amaze her. Even when she was lying to her mom and her friends and dealing with an aching shoulder, it was all worth it for Morgan.

"You're a genius, you know that?" said Kipp.

Morgan looked up from writing on her scratch paper.

"I try," she responded uncertainly.

"Is it hard for you to take compliments?" Kipp asked with a smile. "I don't usually know how to respond to them."

"Fair enough. But don't forget how much you

deserve them."

Morgan rolled her eyes, smiling. "I'll try."

"Hey, how late are you going to be here?" Kipp asked.

"All night. I'm staying here because Amelia doesn't want me somewhere Hall could easily get to."

"That makes sense." Kipp paused, closing the laptop in front of Morgan and leaning in closer. "I have something to tell you."

"Okay?" Morgan let out a small laugh.

"I have a theory about where the big supply of unicorn dust is. When I saw Hall in that abandoned building, I heard them say some names, and two of them were Franklin and Smith, but when I was riding here, I saw that those are actually the names of roads, and on top of that, there's a big warehouse where those roads cross. So, I think something might be going on with that."

"Then why are you telling me? You have to tell Captain Brumbly!"

"I'll tell them as soon as I get here tomorrow. I want to make sure Hall doesn't find out and try to hurt you, or me, because of it."

"How would he find out?"

"If he hacks Amelia's computer, he could."

Morgan glanced at the laptop with unease.

"I promise, the first thing out of my mouth when I get here will be about the warehouse," said Kipp.

"Okay," Morgan relented.

Kipp glanced at the window. It had gotten really

dark. "I should probably get going soon."

"I'll see you tomorrow, then?" Morgan asked.

"Yeah." Kipp smiled.

Morgan stood up to give Kipp a hug. It was like Kipp's whole world froze as she felt Morgan's warmth around her. All her stress and worry dissipated for those few seconds, and it was wonderful.

Kipp hoped she wouldn't hit any roots on the way up her driveway. Maybe she should have tied a headlamp to the front of the bike.

"Where were you? I thought you'd call me," Roberta said when Kipp shut the front door behind her.

"I was doing homework at Luke's house, and then I got a call from Captain Brumbly about the Anthony Hall case, so I went to the precinct. Morgan was trying to crack a code they got in the mail."

"Just make sure to let me know where you are next time."

"I will," Kipp said, starting to walk toward the stairs.

"Hey, hold on. I want to talk to you about something."

"What?"

"This whole case is a pretty big deal, huh?"

"Yeah?"

"I'm just worried about you since you're involved in it. What was that code Morgan working on? Is it for the Hall case?"

"Yeah," Kipp said quietly, turning back to the stairs.

"Hey, tell me about it. How do they know it's connected to the Hall case?"

"Because Morgan got notes like that before, and it talked about stuff that's specific to her before it went into the code."

Roberta hummed, looking down and nodding. The disingenuous smile she wore made Kipp's heart beat faster. "Speaking of Morgan," Roberta said, snapping her head up, "I talked to Captain Brumbly for a little bit, and when I was telling him you had a girlfriend named Morgan, he told me that was pretty funny, since you were talking to a girl named Morgan at the juvie center who's now being taken care of by Amelia Carson."

Kipp was left with her mouth parted and nothing to say. It was rare her mother actually got mad at her for anything. Was she really mad? And what for? Was it more about the 'danger' of Morgan or the fact that Kipp didn't say anything?

"Why didn't you tell me about what Morgan did?" Roberta asked.

"I didn't think it would matter. Did you even ask what happened?"

"Yes, and I really think you should have at least told me about it. She *murdered* someone."

"Because she was attacked!"

Roberta's shoulders were slumped, and her

expression was almost sad. "Baby, it takes a certain kind of person to do something like that."

"Yeah, one that was scared because some random-ass guy tried to assault her when she was *twelve!* And it's not like she's some stone-cold serial killer that looks back on it like, 'Oh yeah, those sure were some good times.' I watched her cry her eyes out just talking about it."

Roberta let out a heavy sigh. "I didn't know she was twelve when it happened, or any context. Brumbly just told me she was in there for murder. I just assumed—"

"What? That she just decided to kill someone for the hell of it?"

"I didn't know! If you just hear that someone killed a person, most people would assume it wasn't under circumstances like that."

"Do you think my judgment is that bad? That I'd just decide to date a person that killed someone for no reason?"

"Okay, okay. You've made your point. I'm not going to say you have to break up with her. All I want you to do is keep you safe. It's my job to worry about you, which is also why I don't want you going to the precinct tomorrow."

Kipp felt her chest sink. "Captain Brumbly told me I need to be there to make sure Morgan is safe."

"That could be really dangerous. I'm sure Morgan will be fine. You're an adult now, I know that, but

I'm not letting you go down there."

"Fine, I'll stay home then." Kipp's voice came out sharp and forceful.

"I'm afraid that won't be enough, and I don't want you tempted to wander off. I'm going to wake up at five thirty tomorrow to pack us some stuff and get you up at six. We're going to go to a hotel and we're going to stay there until the police are sure that those people are gone, or when they've arrested them."

"But how am I going to help? I've been on this case for a long time. Why can't you let me do this one thing? I'm going to be a detective when I grow up anyway, or are you not going to let me do that because it's 'too dangerous?'"

"That's years away! Right now, you aren't a detective. You don't even have a fully developed brain. I'm not letting you risk your life just so you can be involved with this."

"It's not risking my life! Morgan is his target!"

"Morgan's working on the code and you want to be there when it's finished. That means you'll be right near her! What if this Hall person decides he wants to blow up the building she's in or shoot at her through the windows?" Roberta's voice rose to a near-yell. "What is it going to take for you to realize you're going to kill yourself one day doing something reckless like this?"

Kipp's jaw clenched as she let a breath out through

her nose, her wound suddenly deciding to ache. She didn't have time for this, first Nikki, and now her mom. Apparently no one trusted her. Kipp stormed off to her room. It took a heap of her willpower not to slam the door behind her.

Kipp lay on her bed, holding her phone over her face as she looked through all the school emails she never bothered to read. As time passed, she sank lower and lower into the mattress as her eyes continued to glaze over from the mindless scrolling.

Her eyes shot to the door as a quiet knock came from the other side.

"Kipp? Do you want dinner?" her mother asked softly as she slowly opened the door.

"I'm not hungry," Kipp grumbled, looking back to her phone. Roberta stepped closer, eventually sitting down at the end of Kipp's bed.

"Can you look at me? Just for a minute?" Roberta said pleadingly. Kipp finally moved her phone away from her face, and sat up to face her mother. She waited with a small frown for her mother to speak.

"I just want to keep you safe. We've both already lost your dad, and I couldn't live with losing you. You're bright, but you can make rash decisions when you have your mind set on something. I know you wanted to go with the captain to find Hall, but it's dangerous. You're very talented, but you're not invincible," Roberta finished, her eyes never leaving Kipp's.

"I know," Kipp muttered. *I'm not invincible, but I don't have to be to beat Hall.*

She waited until her mom left before setting an alarm for four thirty in the morning and setting out some clothes.

The air was crisp with the lack of sunlight when Kipp quietly shut the front door. Tucked into her pockets were her phone, her taser, and a pair of handcuffs that she'd bought online. She grabbed her bike, which she had left propped up by the stairs, concerned her mom would see or hear the car.

All Kipp could think about while riding was the inconvenience of it all. She should've brought one of her puffy jackets, or at least an extra layer, and it was so dark. She briefly considered turning on her phone's flashlight and trying to prop it up in the bike basket to make sure she didn't hit a rock or something.

Kipp was less than half a mile away from the precinct when she noticed a barely visible figure on the roof of a building pointing an object in her direction. Her confidence was gone in less than a second.

Birds fled the nearby trees as gunshots rang through the air.

Chapter 14

It was nearly nine in the morning when Morgan called to Sergeant Carson that she was finally done with the code.

"Amelia! I figured it out!"

"Great! What's it say?" Amelia asked.

Before Morgan could answer, the sergeant's phone buzzed. Morgan spotted Captain Brumbly's name on the screen.

Amelia picked up the call and her face fell. "Oh my God! Is she okay?" A pause. "Got it." Another pause. "If you'll hold on for a second, Morgan figured out the code. All right." Amelia hit the mute button and turned to Morgan. "Kipp got shot."

Morgan jerked forward, mouth falling open. "What happened?"

"They think it was Hall. There were three shots fired, one missed, the other hit Kipp's shoe, and the last hit her in the arm." Amelia inhaled through her teeth. "Apparently it happened really early this morning, and she lost a lot of blood. The paramedics had to go out and search for Kipp for a little bit because she tried to walk to the hospital. But the doctors did some tests, and it looks like the bullet didn't hit any cause any major damage. Kipp's going to be fine. They said that she might even get released tomorrow afternoon if there's no complications."

"Oh, that's good," Morgan said with a breath of relief. "But why didn't Hall kill her? Whoever shot at her seemed to have the chance. Was it too dark?"

"I don't know. I think someone came out of their house to help, so it must be that the shooter didn't want to risk shooting someone else." Amelia shrugged, looking at the ground.

Morgan hummed in response.

"Sorry I cut you off earlier." Amelia said after a moment. "What does the code say?"

"It says 'ship ship hooray.'" Morgan held up a paper of her work with *Ship Ship Hooray* written and circled at the bottom as her final conclusion.

"Well, that's weird."

"Yes, it is," Morgan agreed. "I can look it up to see if I can find something."

Amelia nodded, taking the phone off mute. "Are you still there? Yeah, it says 'ship ship hooray.' Morgan is going to look up what it means. I'll tell you when she finds something." She handed the phone to Morgan with the captain still on the line. From typing *ship ship hooray* into Safari, Morgan found nothing that seemed to be related to the case at first. But she only had to scroll for a second before she found something that caught her eye.

"I think I found something," she said. The captain was silent on the other end, waiting. "There was this serial killer, Dr. Harold Shipman, that would kill his elderly patients. A newspaper headline when he died was Ship Ship Hooray. It looks like he killed a *lot* of people. He would kill them by…" Morgan's voice faded out as she stared at the screen. "By giving them morphine overdoses," she finished. Her eyes grew wider, her voice growing loud and frantic. "Morphine sulfate is given through an IV! Kipp's injury would need an IV!" Morgan shot up from her seat.

"Calm down. We don't know that—" Amelia tried.

"Call the police, call the hospital, have someone in Kipp's room that she knows! Do something!" Morgan shook the phone in front of Amelia for her to grab. The sergeant immediately hung up with Captain Brumbly, figuring it would be faster to have an officer closer to the hospital deal with it. She was just starting to dial 911 when Morgan sprinted out of the room.

"Morgan, stop! Someone stop her!" Amelia yelled. Morgan fell to the ground right outside the front door as she was tackled by an officer.

"No, no, no! Let me go, it's an emergency!"

Morgan cried, desperately squirming in the officer's hold.

A crowd of people began to gather outside, including the sergeant, who was on the line with police dispatch. Morgan stopped struggling, and went quiet. The officer tried to lift her up, but she was completely limp. Amelia stepped closer, phone clutched nervously in her hand. Morgan seemed to be conscious, staring at her with wide eyes filled to the brim with terror.

"Morgan? What's wrong?" the sergeant asked. Silence. The officer gasped as a bead of blood rolled down Morgan's neck from a wound that none of them had inflicted.

Chapter 15

Nikki's hands were clamped around the steering wheel, her whole body tense as she drove to the hospital. Isabel sat in the passenger seat and Luke in the back.

"I'm sure Kipp will be fine," said Luke, nervously picking at his already chipped black nail polish. "They said the wound wasn't as bad as it could have been."

"It's a *gunshot wound!*" Nikki said in return. "I should've just called her mom, or went over there, or something! Then there'd at least be a chance that this wouldn't happen."

"Try not to blame yourself too much," Isabel said, barely above a whisper.

They rode in silence the rest of the way without so much as music to cover up their nervous breaths.

"Hi, we're here to see our friend Kipp Green," Nikki stated to the receptionist when they finally made it to the hospital.

"I've been given a list of people allowed to visit her." She typed away before looking up from her computer. "Names?"

"Nicole Young."

"Lucas Tompson."

"Isabel Viera."

"I see you're all on the list. Do you have some form of identification?" asked the receptionist. After inspecting their driver's licenses, the receptionist gave them the room number.

The friends were walking toward the room when a group of police officers flew past them. The group exchanged worried glances, and Nikki's heart sank as the officers entered Kipp's room. Nikki broke into a run, followed by Isabel and Luke. They stopped at the door, and a man wearing a nurse outfit and a medical mask came running out, holding a bag of fluid, followed by two of the three officers. They all sprinted down the hall. Nikki peeked into the room, where a thin officer with light brown hair was standing by a confused and disoriented Kipp. The nametag on his uniform read *C. Jordan.*

"What's going on?" Kipp slurred as she tried to sit up in the hospital bed.

"You're going to be okay, Kipp, but the doctors recommend that you go back to sleep for a little while," Officer Jordan said calmly. Kipp obliged and slowly laid back down, not noticing her friends in the doorway. Another officer and a nurse approached the kids at the door.

"Are you friends of Kipp?" asked the nurse.

"Yes. Can we see her?" Nikki said quickly.

"No. She needs to rest. She'll probably be awake and cleared for visitors by two, but we just had someone try to attack her, so the last thing we need is a bunch of people in here. We really just need space to do our jobs right now."

"Can you at least tell us what happened? What do you mean someone tried to attack her?"

"You need to go," the officer said firmly. He stepped in front of the nurse, blocking the door.

"Can you *please* tell us what happened?" Nikki was ready to shake the officer by his shoulders.

"There was some attempted tampering with her IV," the officer said flatly. "Now you need to go somewhere else. Stay in the waiting room, go to the cafeteria, or just go home. Just go anywhere but here."

"Okay." Nikki let out a heavy exhale. "We'll be back at two."

The group turned around and started walking toward the elevators.

"This is insane," Luke said as they stepped into the elevator.

"Yeah," Nikki agreed.

"What do you think happened?" asked Isabel.

"Hall," Nikki said with a sour tone.

They stood silently as the elevator ascended to the

second floor. Nikki couldn't think of anything to say as Luke glanced around while Isabel stared at her shoes. The doors opened and they all got off and followed the signs pointing them to the cafeteria.

They made their way to the buffet. After filling their plates, they sat down at one of the small wooden tables in the near-empty cafeteria. No one looked up from their food for a while.

"The food is kind of cold. I mean, it's not awful, but it's not great," Luke said into the silence.

Nikki stared at her plate with her head in her hands. Why didn't she just tell Kipp's mom about the walk the day it happened? She could feel her eyes getting hot.

"Are you okay?" Luke asked.

Nikki shook her head. She felt Isabel's hand come to rest on her shoulder.

Kipp opened her eyes to light streaming into the white hospital room.

"Kipp," a soft voice said. A blonde nurse was standing over her. "You have some visitors."

Kipp turned her head to see Nikki, Isabel, and Luke standing in the doorway. She smiled. "Hey everybody!"

"Hey!" said Luke

"Hi!" Isabel waved.

"How are you doing?" Nikki asked, walking over to the bed.

"Pretty good. I feel a lot better," Kipp replied.

"Where's your mom?" asked Nikki.

"I don't know." Kipp looked down at the sheets, interlacing her fingers. "She'll probably be here soon." *Unless she's at that hotel or something. Where I should've been.*

"I guess you're stuck with us until she gets here," said Luke.

"Oh no, someone get me out of here!" Kipp wailed before breaking into laughter.

"So what happened?" Nikki asked when everyone went quiet.

When Kipp was finished retelling the story, she paused to look around at everyone. Her gaze paused on Nikki, not being able to pin down her expression. It was uncomfortably close to the disappointed look she so rarely got from her mother.

"How does your arm feel?"

"Fine. It hurts, but I'm on some painkillers." She swallowed. "I have to tell you guys something."

Isabel and Luke leaned forward, but Nikki's posture straightened as her expression softened.

"What?" Isabel asked.

"Something happened when Nikki and I were on a walk. Someone that was connected to Hall shot at me. That's why I fell off the bridge. That was kind of an important life event, so I probably should've told you sooner, but I didn't want you to freak out or anything."

Isabel glanced at Nikki before talking. "Thanks for telling us."

Luke nodded in agreement and silence overtook the room.

"Why would Hall want to hurt you?" Isabel asked.

"After I saw him in an abandoned building a few months ago, I got two of his dealers arrested recently, and then I helped the police find a storage locker with a bunch of drugs. And I also think I might know where he's hiding a bunch more."

"Did you tell the police about where you think that hiding place is?" asked Nikki.

"No." Kipp knocked her head against the pillow. "I was planning to tell Captain Brumbly today. I was supposed to be at the precinct this morning to help keep Morgan safe."

Luke sat down in a chair in the corner of the room "Why didn't you want to tell us?"

"I was afraid you guys would be roped into the case and be put in danger."

"I get that," said Luke. It was silent for a few seconds. "Does anyone want some Jello from the cafeteria?"

In the middle of the group quietly eating their Jello, the hospital room's door opened. Kipp whipped to face the door with wide eyes, her grip on the plastic spoon tightening. Captain Brumbly stepped inside.

"Hi Kipp, it's great to see you're feeling better."

"Thanks," Kipp said, exhaling. "Hey, do you

know where my mom is? I haven't seen her at all since before I was in the hospital."

"Yes. Some of Hall's men broke into your house after you left. Luckily she was able to get out before they found her, and she called 911. We've arrested one of them, but the other two got away. Roberta is staying at the precinct for her own safety."

"Oh." Kipp couldn't get any other reaction out. Had she really just chosen the Hall case over her own mother? She should've been there. Her mom had probably been scared to death to wake up and find her gone and then people breaking into the house.

"We haven't told her what happened yet," the captain explained. "We're worried that she'll try to leave the precinct to come see you and be targeted by some of Hall's lackeys. We told her that you're staying at a hotel and that we didn't want to risk transporting you right away,"

"Do we have to tell her that I was in the hospital?" Kipp asked cautiously.

"We're going to have to do that eventually, even if you don't," the captain stated. Kipp could already hear the scolding words of her mother: the frantic, worried voice that would make her heart ache with regret. Those thoughts were interrupted as a new one popped into her head,

"Did Morgan ever figure out what the code said?"

"Yes, it said 'ship ship hooray.'" Brumbly explained

the article that Morgan had found and how she had connected it to Kipp being in the hospital. "The police got here just in time to find one of Anthony's people trying to switch your IV with one of pure morphine. It would have killed you."

"Holy shit." Kipp smiled despite the shame she felt. "I… I'll have to get Morgan a present or something when I see her again. I really hope she goes on to be a detective, or in the FBI or something."

"I agree. She'd make an excellent investigator," the captain seconded. His smile never reached his eyes, and that made Kipp feel even worse.

Kipp nodded, letting her smile drop a little. That was three times now where she could've died. Her mom was right. She had to pull it together. No more stupid decisions. No more big arguments with Nikki. And when she could talk to her mom, she would tell her everything that happened and that she wouldn't do it again in a million years.

The next day, Kipp was given her belongings as well as some clothes that her friends had brought from her house.

"I brought a bulletproof vest for you. You can wear it as a precaution and we'll be able to take you to your mom," the captain announced, pulling a black vest from his bag. "You can get your things together, and I'll drive you to the precinct."

"Thanks. I do want to tell her about the whole

being-shot thing myself, though."

"All right. We'll get out of here so you can get dressed." Brumbly backed out of the room, Kipp's friends following him.

"After I do, I have something to tell you about the case!" she called.

"Okay, I'll be waiting right out here." Brumbly closed the door.

Kipp grabbed her folded clothes from the end of the bed and quickly pulled them on, grateful to whichever of her friends had picked them out. Clearly they'd been prioritizing comfort, being that they'd brought a pair of sweatpants, a T-shirt, and a sweatshirt.

After strapping the vest into place, Kipp lifted her phone from the windowsill. She planned on quickly going through Instagram to see what she'd missed yesterday, then emailing her lacrosse coach to profusely apologize for having to miss practice again; however, a single text notification caught her attention. It was sent by a number she didn't recognize.

She clicked on the video they'd sent. It began to play, the audio popping with static sounds, and Kipp could see that it was filmed from a rooftop. She saw a long object that resembled the barrel of a gun appear in the corner of the screen when a figure came into view, exiting a nearby building. Kipp quickly realized the building was the police station, and the figure was so familiar.

"*Morgan,*" Kipp breathed. She watched as Morgan was tackled by a cop that was apparently chasing her. The officer shifted, and the gun in the corner of the frame jerked as if it had been fired, a quiet sound emitting from it.

The cop tried to pull Morgan up by her arms, but she didn't move. She wasn't *moving.* Kipp's breathing quickened, her eyes glued to Morgan's limp form. Although Kipp couldn't see Morgan's face, she saw the reactions of the people surrounding her. One person stepped back and clapped a hand over their mouth, people started to yell and a few ran back inside.

Kipp's heart sank down to her feet. *She's dead. She's dead. She's dead.* A wrenching feeling went through her chest as if she had almost fallen down a flight of stairs. It was followed by a sensation of absolute emptiness.

She crumpled to the ground, slouching under the weight of what she'd just witnessed. Her head fell into her hands as she fought back the tears glossing over her eyes. She let out a quiet sob. It wasn't long before she had made marks with her fingernails from squeezing her hands into fists. *They fucking killed her.* The video was sent a while ago. Captain Brumbly *must* have known about this. And he didn't tell her? Did he just not want to get her worked up? Her girlfriend was *dead*, and he was trying to keep it from her. How *could* he?

She pushed herself to her feet, and only then did she allow her emotions to fully transition from sorrow to pure wrath. *I'm going to beat the fucking shit out of Hall right before I send him to rot in a cell for the rest of his miserable fucking life!* She snatched up her taser and handcuffs, a hot tear running down her cheek.

By the time someone went in to check on Kipp, she was long gone, the window left open and a small breeze blowing through.

The captain and the group of friends looked around the room, as if Kipp could have been hiding somewhere, ready to pop out and tell them it was all a joke.

"Where would she be going?" said Captain Brumbly.

"She might've gone to try and find Hall," said Nikki. The captain cursed under his breath, pinching his nose bridge.

"Then we'll have to find her as soon as possible." He stepped out, already dialing a number on his phone.

"I'm going to go after her," Nikki whispered to Isabel and Luke as they all walked away from the captain, who had just gotten on the phone. "I'll call you and tell you where we are, and you can call the police if I find her."

"But—" Isabel tried to protest.

"You guys *stay here*!" Nikki said before running toward the elevators. She was not going to let Kipp hurt herself again.

Chapter 16

Kipp looked for any sign of Hall or his associates as she marched toward the warehouse. Her eyes were teary with anger, though she made sure to wipe them away the second they spilled over. She stared at the side door, preparing to run in.

Just then, she heard a voice behind her.

"Kipp, wait up!"

Adrenaline shot through her, but she quickly recognized Nikki's voice. "Why did you follow me?" Kipp turned around, tucking her tightly curled hands into her pockets.

"Why did *you* go after a drug lord and his gang that wants to kill you? Huh? I followed you to make sure you weren't going to do anything else stupid."

"He killed my girlfriend."

"Wait, wait, wait, wait. He killed Morgan? How do you know?"

"I watched her get shot. That sadistic asshole sent me a *video* of it. You shouldn't have followed me."

Kipp teeth were pressed together hard enough to snap a jawbreaker. She forced her jaw to relax.

"I'm… so sorry. I can't…" her voice trailed off. "I can't believe it. Kipp, I'm so sorry." Nikki pulled Kipp into a hug. Although Kipp didn't put her arms around Nikki, she hung her head so it rested on her shoulder. Suddenly, Nikki pulled away. "We need to go to the precinct, like, right now! You're in so much danger right now. I will drag you out of here if I have to." She grabbed Kipp's hand and yanked it, but turned to see a large group of men walking around the side of the warehouse. Many were holding guns, some had stern expressions, and others were smiling.

Kipp could only mouth the words 'oh shit'. Minutes ago, she'd been ready to tear Hall apart, but Nikki was here now. Nikki had no bulletproof vest, no training, and no wrath fueling her confidence. Kipp couldn't lose her too.

A man in a dark suit stepped out from the group, a pistol in his hand. He raised a hand to scratch the dark stubble on his chin. His brown hair was greasy with something he'd smeared over it to slick it back. Cold green eyes stared back at Kipp without an ounce of mercy in them.

"Look at that. The arrogant little pest Kipp Green," he sneered with a smile full of malice.

"Anthony Hall," Kipp muttered through gritted teeth. Her stomach began to twist into knots. Out of the corner of her eye, she saw Nikki put her hands behind her back, slowly pulling her phone out of her back pocket.

"I see you brought a friend," Hall said, attention turning to Nikki. Kipp stared at him, her eyes filled with fury and her fists clenched. Nikki moved her hands in front of her, phone hidden in her sleeve.

"Are you ready to go live in a concrete box for the rest of your life?" Kipp asked, effectively hiding her unsteady breathing.

"Oh, no, I don't think that's going to happen," Hall replied, still smiling.

"Why are you so sure?"

"I've been doing this longer than you've been alive. I know when I've won."

"And you were calling *me* arrogant."

"I hope you know that all of this could've been avoided if you had just gone home the day you saw us in this building. But now you've seen our faces, and it won't do to have you pick any of us out in a lineup."

Kipp stole a glance at Nikki once again. She was looking at her sleeve, tapping at something inside of it.

Kipp started to hear some static-like noise. Nikki must've bumped the speaker mode button.

Isabel's voice rang out through the phone hidden in her sleeve. "Hello? Are you there? Where are you?"

Hall's attention snapped back to Nikki.

"Warehouse," Nikki hissed down toward the phone.

"What do you have there?" Hall's lanky form sauntered over to Nikki as her face drained of color. Kipp couldn't protest as Hall stopped not a foot away from her friend. It was like she could feel suffering radiating off of him, threatening to be released onto her or Nikki if she made one wrong move.

"I'm going to have to ask you to hand that over to me." He grabbed Nikki's wrist, snatching the phone out of her sleeve with his other hand. Dropping the phone onto the ground, Hall lifted his foot, and with a solid stomp, cracked it to no repair. With a dismissive huff of laughter, he turned to face Kipp.

She had to come up with something to say to take the attention off of Nikki. "Took your goons long enough to finally hit me. You guys have *terrible* aim."

"Those were only meant to scare you. But clearly, you never took the warnings. As for the code and the attempted morphine overdose, I would have liked that to work, however, Morgan Toner was quicker to solve the code than I expected. She would have had to live her life with the guilt of your death, believing that it was all her fault. That would have been pretty funny."

Kipp dug her nails into her palms. "Maybe you just recruit people with really bad aim and make really bad plans," she responded, trying her best not to let her fists shake.

"My employee's aim was fine with Toner. Maybe she'd still be alive if she didn't try to run and help you," Hall said with an apathetic laugh. Kipp felt as if she was about to explode from the pent up rage boiling inside of her. "Did you enjoy the video? I thought it'd be a nice idea."

"You're fucked up, you know that?" Kipp spat.

"Am I? Judging by her track record, Morgan was a lot more unstable than me."

"You're a fucking psycho. You killed her for no reason."

"She also killed someone. However, *her* crime was far more brutal. That man died from blood loss in a dingy alley because your friend stabbed him in the neck. At least I was kind enough to give her a quick and painless death." Something more like a giggle than a laugh bubbled from Hall's throat. "Hey, if you want to invite me to the funeral, I might let you live."

"Guess I'll die, then." Kipp said, her unsteady voice weighed down with emotion. The smile Hall gave her made Kipp want to punch him until all of his teeth fell out. She used the back of her hand to brush away a tear that had fallen.

"Aw, is someone sad?" Hall mocked in a voice like he was talking to a toddler.

"Shut the fuck up," Kipp hissed.

"You should follow your own advice," Hall said, raising his pistol. Kipp froze, but Hall moved his aim before quickly firing.

A cry of pain sent Kipp's stomach plummeting. She jerked her head over just in time to see Nikki's knee buckle beneath her.

"Nikki!" Kipp screamed as panic pumped through her veins.

"Somehow you're convinced you're invincible: special in some way," Hall said, slowly raising the pistol. "I, on the other hand, see you as what you are: a dumb kid in over her head. You've stuck your nose into way too much of my business, and I'm sure you've heard of that old saying… curiosity killed the cat."

Kipp froze, her eyes locked on the weapon.

"Don't—" Nikki strained to say, but was interrupted by Hall.

"Shut up," he said firmly, pointing the gun at Nikki.

"Leave her alone!" Kipp cried.

Hall smirked. "I'll think about it." He cocked the gun, aiming the muzzle right in the middle of Kipp's forehead.

She squeezed her eyes shut, taking in shuddering breaths. She was going to die. Nikki would be alone with them, but maybe the police would get there in time. Her mom would be devastated. All her friends, too. But hey, if there was an afterlife she'd be able to see Morgan and her dad. If not, at least she wouldn't have to feel pain before she was dropped into the dark abyss of death.

A shot rang out and Kipp flinched. She waited, but she was still conscious, and there was no pain.

She heard a few murmurs of shock, and snapped her eyes open to see Hall on the ground with a pool of blood forming around his head. The group of men drew their weapons, the ones without already starting to back away. Captain Brumbly breathed laboriously as he held his arm out the window of his squad car, his gun still aimed at where Hall had stood.

Sirens began to wail in the distance. It wasn't long before the red and blue lights came into view. The group of men immediately began shooting at the police cars as they started to scatter in different directions, many of them rushing into the woods. Dozens of police cars pulled up in front of them, along with an ambulance, and officers immediately jumped out and began to pursue.

Kipp ran over to Nikki who groaned in pain as she tried to readjust her leg.

"Nik, I'm so sorry. This is my fault. I should've never gone out here. Then none of this would've happened. I'm so sorry," she said, chest tightening in guilt.

"Just don't be this much of a dumbass again," Nikki said, mustering a smile. Kipp didn't force herself to smile back.

"I won't. I promise," she pledged. Kipp was shooed

away as Nikki was lifted onto a stretcher and taken toward the ambulance. Hall's associates were well into the distance by now, a few being walked back to the scene in handcuffs as gunshots still sounded in the air. One car caught Kipp's eye. It wasn't an emergency vehicle, and Kipp soon recognized it as Sergeant Carson's car. The passenger door was flung open, and to Kipp's utter dismay, out stepped Morgan Toner, who rested her hand on the side of the car, looking as if she was going to collapse from relief. Kipp quickly wiped a tear starting to fall from her eye.

"I thought you were dead," she said.

"Why did you think that?" Morgan tilted her head at Kipp, who had started to cautiously walk closer, as if approaching a ghost.

"Someone sent me a video of you outside the precinct and it looked like they shot you. You weren't moving."

"I *was* shot at. It barely grazed the side of my neck and it was just enough to bleed, so I stayed still until everyone brought me inside to clean and bandage the wound. They called the paramedics and had them leave with a sheet over the stretcher so it'd look like I was dead," Morgan explained.

"I guess some of them were just bad shots," Kipp mumbled under her breath.

Sergeant Carson had exited the car by that point, and came to stand next to her. They all watched as the men that had been caught were directed into police vehicles, sneers etched into their faces.

As the cars started to pull away, Kipp looked back to Morgan and Amelia and rushed over. Morgan had no time to react before Kipp flung her arms around her, lifting Morgan off her feet in a tight embrace. She had to set her down soon after as the pain from her arm and shoulder became almost unbearable. Kipp gazed down at her girlfriend, wishing she could hold her for hours. The affection she felt for Morgan in that moment was overwhelming. She couldn't have been more grateful that both of them were alive. Pink glowed on Morgan's cheeks as she looked up at Kipp, breaking eye contact every few seconds. Kipp took Morgan's face in her hands and their eyes settled on each other.

"I'm so glad you're okay," Kipp whispered. "I don't think I'll ever be able to thank you enough. I mean, you literally saved my life with that hospital thing."

Morgan smiled, putting her hands on Kipp's. "Oh!" Morgan exclaimed, pulling away. "We found out how Hall knew about my research!"

"That's great! How'd you do it?"

Morgan looked at Sergent Carson.

Amelia scoffed. "It made me so mad. After I knew Morgan was safe, I went back into the meeting room to get my stuff, but when I picked up the bear that Davey gave Morgan, I saw something weird about the eye. Turns out the bear had a camera and microphone in it. I had told Davey about *everything*. We couldn't find him anywhere, so he probably skipped town, but we'll catch him eventually—"

"Kipp!" Roberta's voice cut through the air as she nearly fell trying to get out of the back of Brumbly's car. Kipp turned to Morgan one last time.

"I should probably go to my mom. I'll see you soon." She flashed her a lopsided smile before dashing off to meet her mother. Roberta ran to her, nearly knocking Kipp over as she wrapped her daughter in a crushing hug. She let out a teary sigh of relief. When Roberta pulled back, they could both see the tears glinting in the other's eyes. Kipp had honestly been terrified. She had never been more grateful to see her mother's face.

"Honey, I'm so glad you're safe," she breathed.

"I'm so sorry. I thought I could handle everything, and I put Nikki in danger, and—"

"Kipp, hey, it's okay. I can tell that you've learned from this, and now you won't make those mistakes again. It's okay. I'm just glad you're safe."

Kipp gave a watery smile in return.

Chapter 17

Two weeks later, Kipp invited Morgan on a picnic to celebrate their survival of the ordeal. Kipp drove them to a place she would occasionally go running. It was a modestly sized field filled with small flowers and nearly surrounded by woods, which had a network of overgrown trails. A small pond sat close by, next to a large oak tree.

As they exited the car, Morgan began to open the door to the backseat.

"Nope. I'm getting the bag." Kipp immediately stuck her arm in front of Morgan and grabbed the backpack, throwing it over her shoulders.

"Are you sure? Because I'd be fine carrying it."

"I got it," Kipp assured.

"Okay. Let me know if you want me to take it. If your shoulders get tired or anything."

"Don't worry." Kipp turned to face Morgan and swung her arm under Morgan's legs, the other staying under her torso as she scooped her into a bridal carry. "My shoulders are fine." Morgan tucked her arms into her chest, looking up as Kipp smiled down at her.

The field was now fully in view from the mulch path that led to it. The grass was tall, and colorful wildflowers stood out against the vast green. After a moment, Morgan draped her arms around Kipp's neck as she carried her into the grass.

She gently set Morgan down before sliding the backpack off, setting it on the ground, and laying out on the blanket. The cloud that had been blocking the sun had moved, bathing them in light as they set out the plates. Kipp had packed sandwiches and lemonade, which she poured into plastic wine glasses and set on a tray that she brought. They ate and drank while birds sang in the trees, the melodies drifting softly through the air.

"How's the sandwich?" Kipp asked as Morgan set the uneaten half back into the wrap.

"Good, I just get full quickly. I'll have more in a minute."

"That's fine. I can put it back in the bag so it doesn't get pollen or anything on it. Let me know when you want more."

"Thank you, I will," Morgan replied.

The blanket shifted a bit as Kipp lay back, placing her hands behind her head. "When I was little, I loved looking at clouds and seeing what shapes they made. I don't do that a lot anymore, but sometimes

I just like looking."

"Yeah," said Morgan. She laid back beside Kipp, folding her hands over her stomach and looking to the sky.

"I used to come here with my dad. We'd go fishing in that pond over there." She pointed to the small body of water. "I'd always get tired of waiting for the fish to bite and he'd bribe me with ice cream. We always stayed until I got a fish and then we'd throw it back and go home."

"That sounds nice. I would be too scared to touch the worms. I'd feel bad putting them on the hook."

"Yeah, that wasn't my favorite part."

"I meant to ask if your arm was okay after carrying everything." Morgan sat up a little to make eye contact with Kipp.

"Oh, don't worry about it. It's healed a lot. C'mere," Kipp said, reaching out her arms and making a motion with her hands like a child grabbing for a toy. Morgan moved closer and laid down, resting her head under Kipp's neck. "I'm so glad I get to go to prom with you. And just to live long enough to be here with you at all." She rested her arms on Morgan's back.

Morgan pressed her own arms to Kipp's sides. "I'm glad I'm here too."

The next day, Morgan went with Amelia to a formal wear shop to find a prom dress. Morgan fixed her eyes onto the deep blue floor, trying to distance herself from the memories that threatened to surface as she caught a glimpse of what looked like hundreds of pink dresses on racks near the front.

"Do you need help finding something?" Amelia asked. "We can ask someone that works here to help you pick out some things."

"I think I'll just walk around."

"Okay, I'll follow you."

Morgan's vision ran over the long pieces of fabric as she walked around the store. She pulled out a few that were mildly appealing to her, one a plain silky burgundy, another navy with a high neck, and the last one turquoise with rhinestone detail all over the bodice. Her eyes suddenly snagged on a black dress. She walked over, gaze unwilling to move anywhere else, and took it off the rack.

"I think I'm done looking," Morgan said, readjusting her hold on the dresses.

"Let's find a dressing room. I think they're in the back," said Amelia.

Morgan ducked into one of the wooden cubicles and hung the dresses on the hanger.

She was quick to find that the burgundy dress was too big.

Amelia's voice came from the other side of the curtain. "Hey, come out and show me once you get it on. I won't try to convince you which one to get or anything. I just want to see."

"This one is too big. I don't think I can come out with it on."

"Oh. Do you want me to ask for another size?"

"No, it's okay. I didn't like the color as much as I thought I would." She tossed the dress over the top of the curtain rod and began putting on the next dress. She found that the turquoise one gapped in some places and had a slit down the side that was uncomfortably high for her liking. Nevertheless, she stepped out of the fitting room.

"Oh, that's pretty. What do you think of it?" asked Amelia.

"I don't like how high this goes," Morgan answered, pointing to the slit that began right below her hip bone, quickly walking back inside.

She had higher hopes for the dark blue dress. It fit well enough, and when she came out of the dressing room, she found it flattered her quite nicely. However, after standing in it for a minute, she noticed that the high neck seemed to be getting tighter by the second. Once back in the dressing room, she gratefully unzipped it, rubbing her neck to soothe it.

Finally, she turned to the black dress. She slipped it on, smiling as she found it didn't gap or slip off. Her lips parted as she stepped out and looked in the mirror. It had lace detail at the hem as well as the neckline with off-the-shoulder straps that clung to the sides of her shoulders. It was a little long, but that could be fixed with some heels.

"Ooh, I think that's my favorite," said Amelia. "How do you feel about it?"

"I like it. I *really* like it, but it feels weird to think about actually wearing it somewhere." *They're gone.* Morgan's eyes locked with her reflection. *They're gone.* She swallowed, holding her breath to keep her heart rate under control.

They're gone. It's my fault. She closed her eyes and inhaled.

It's my fault.

Stop it.

It's my fault.

Shut up! Morgan let her breath out and turned back around, facing the sergeant. *Whether they deserved how they died or not, they don't deserve to affect me now.*

"You don't have to wear a dress if you don't want to. Do you want to try and look for a nice blouse or something?" Amelia offered.

"No, I'm okay." She exhaled slowly, smiling as she looked at herself in the mirror. "I want to keep the dress."

A burnt stench filled Luke's bathroom as curling irons and straighteners were heated to their highest settings. Kipp delicately wrapped strands of hair around the wand, carefully avoiding touching her fingers to the scalding metal. Her stomach had been doing flips for the last few days in anticipation. After many times scrubbing off crooked liner, she finally got it even on both eyes. Kipp brushed on some deep red lipstick and squeezed past Nikki, who was in the middle of patting blush onto her cheeks while trying to instruct Luke on how to properly put on eyeliner.

"I'm going to go pick up Morgan," said Kipp.

"Don't go in without us!" Nikki called as Kipp got to the door.

She smiled back at Nikki. "I won't." Kipp walked to her car and took a deep breath before starting the engine. She smiled thinking of the night ahead, not bothering to test the brakes and horn before driving off.

Kipp stepped into Sergeant Carson's house with shiny dress shoes and an impeccably ironed suit. Morgan was waiting on the other side of the door, hands fidgeting with each other. She looked so pretty, and every feature was accentuated by her happiness. The dress fit her perfectly, and her makeup made her eyes shine like bright blue marbles.

"Hey— Whoa! You look amazing!" Kipp exclaimed.

"You look amazing too." Morgan's smile widened.

"Are you ready to head out?" Kipp asked.

"Yes. I'm ready."

"Great, let's go!" Kipp theatrically stuck out her arm, and Morgan smiled as she took hold of it. As they approached the car, Kipp broke away to open the passenger door for Morgan before rounding the car and getting in the driver's seat.

The music from the hotel ballroom the school had rented could be heard from outside the door. Morgan prepared to shove her fingers in her ears, but the sounds didn't overwhelm her like she'd expected. The freshly waxed wood floors shined, reflecting the dim lights from the ceiling. She and Kipp had arrived fashionably late and met Kipp's friends outside. They all took their commemorative picture and made their way inside, to the food table.

"These look pretty good," Luke said, plucking a cake square from one of the trays.

"I heard someone's parents offered to make some of the snacks this year," Nikki said as she adjusted the crutches she was forced to use until her knee healed. Her date, Cameron, took a mini brownie off the table and held it to her lips, allowing her to eat it without putting her crutches down.

"Everyone looks great!" Isabel exclaimed, "I've been so excited for senior prom. We can finally be as fancy as we want!"

"Yeah, Morgan, I love your dress," Nikki commented with a smile.

"Thanks! Yours looks great too," said Morgan. She could feel Kipp's smile on her as she beamed. The compliment gave her even more confidence. Amelia had taken the time to give her a surprisingly well-done smoky-eye. She'd added dark lip gloss and a small bit of concealer under her eyes. It had been almost six years since she had worn makeup, and it was refreshing to look in the mirror and see it on her face without bruises covered up by ghostly pale foundation.

"We're going to go say hi to Cameron's friends but we'll be back," said Nikki. She and Cameron melted into the crowd.

"Guys, come on, let's go dance!" Luke motioned for everyone to join him as he walked toward the floor, swinging his arms in the air.

"Yeah!" Isabel followed him onto the floor.

Holding a cup of lemonade, Morgan scanned the room as she rubbed the back of her neck. Kipp's words pulled her attention away.

"You want to dance?" she asked.

"I don't really know how. I feel like I'd embarrass myself," Morgan laughed a little.

"Oh, come on. You definitely won't be the worst one out there." Kipp was quick to notice how Morgan uncomfortably eyed the dance floor once more.

"If you really want to, then—" Morgan began. Kipp quickly interrupted her with another offer.

"How about we wait until a slow song comes on? Most people either square dance or just spin around with each other. It's super easy and everyone will be too busy focused on each other than to look at us. Would you like that better?"

Morgan smiled and nodded, letting out the tension she was holding in her chest.

They waited, talking and eating until a slower song finally played. Morgan drew in a breath as Kipp led her onto the floor, trying to undo the knots her stomach was tying itself into. Once the two were situated on the floor where they weren't at risk of hitting another couple, Kipp placed a hand on the small of Morgan's back, closing the other around Morgan's hand. Morgan unsurely placed her other hand on Kipp's shoulder blade. Soft smiles adorned both of their faces as they began to sway, taking small steps back and forth.

The entire world disappeared for Kipp and Morgan as they danced slowly in their small space on the floor. Their histories retreated to the backs of their minds, and their worries faded away, all their attention focused on each other's eyes. After the song ended, the couple simply stood there for a moment, unmoving as the low yellow lights from the ceiling reflected in their eyes. Even as the memories of her parents screaming and the cold air conditioning at the NJC materialized in the back of Morgan's mind, it didn't make her hesitate.

Another song started and Morgan looked away from Kipp's softly burning gaze. The two made their way off the floor. They spent the rest of the night conversing with Kipp's friends and Kipp bringing Morgan through many introductions. Occasionally, everyone would rush to the floor to dance to a familiar song, except Morgan, who was content to watch on the sidelines and clap along.

As everyone filtered out of the venue, Kipp and Morgan made their way to Kipp's car as everyone filtered out of the venue. Kipp drove through the darkness to drop Morgan back at Amelia's house. She walked with her up the porch and waited as Morgan unlocked the door, but Morgan turned around before opening it.

"That was one of the most fun things I've ever done. Thank you so much for inviting me." Morgan felt a giddy energy course through her as she looked up at Kipp with a wide smile.

"No problem. I've been to homecoming and prom, but never with anyone, and I can safely say you going with me made it a lot better." She reached to tuck a strand of hair behind Morgan's ear.

Again, their gazes locked, unmoving. Morgan felt her heart surge with a mix of anxiety, anticipation, and excitement when Kipp's eyes flicked down to her lips. Her breath became unsteady and she began to feel her heart thump against her ribs before she mustered up the courage to lean forward a little bit. Kipp met her halfway.

Both of their lips tasted vaguely sweet from the lemonade and punch they'd drunk not long ago. Kipp brought a hand up to cradle Morgan's cheek, followed by Morgan lightly resting her hands on

Kipp's shoulders.

Blushes adorned their cheeks as they slowly pulled away from each other.

"Um, goodnight," Morgan squeaked, grabbing the door handle sheepishly.

"Goodnight," Kipp said softly. Her girlfriend waved before shutting the door.

Kipp sighed dreamily as she made her way back down the sidewalk, feeling like she was walking on a cloud. As she walked down the dark street and approached her car, though, she felt a small twinge of dread in the pit of her stomach.

Her walk slowed with every step she took until she was standing only feet from her car, just watching. She had parked on the curb about half a block away from Amelia's house. People would hear her if she screamed, right? *Jesus, Kipp, walk forward. Your car is right there.*

Stomach squeezing in protest, she walked over to the driver's side door, but as soon as she rounded the car, the person that was ducked down and leaning against the door came into view.

Chapter 18

Kipp yelled in shock, rearing back. There was a man crouched beside the door, clutching a dirty crowbar that looked like it had been buried for years. He stood up abruptly. Kipp considered running around the car to get in on the other side. She decided against it. The man would probably be able to break the window and open the door before she could even get in the driver's seat.

"Fuck," she hissed. Although he was steady on his feet, the man looked high out of his mind. Kipp could just barely make out a bit of white powder stuck in his mustache. Adjusting the metal in his hand, he took a threatening step forward.

"Give me any money you have and the keys to the car," he demanded.

"No." Kipp resisted the urge to add on a phrase challenging the man to come and get them himself.

"Give them to me now, and you won't get hurt," the man growled.

"Get the hell away from my car!" Kipp yelled. Hopefully Sergeant Carson would hear and come out to arrest this guy.

The man took long, fast strides toward Kipp, who backed up. He swung the bar down, and Kipp dodged it, but the next one came fast, and she opted to grab onto the bar instead.

She hung on as the man thrashed around, trying to loosen her grip enough to rip it away. "Someone call the police!" she yelled even louder this time, fearing that if she gave up the crowbar to get to her phone, he would hit her. Kipp felt a bit of relief as she heard a door open, but when she turned around for a split second she could see it wasn't Carson that stepped out to aid her.

Morgan stood on the porch with a knife held unsteadily in her hands. Kipp turned around again, meeting Morgan's eyes. "Call the cops!" Her heart dropped as the bar was torn from her grasp. The second she turned her head back to face the man, the metal cracked against her nose.

The pain jabbed past the bridge of her nose into her skull and she stumbled back, watching as blood dribbled onto her white dress shirt. Morgan had stepped off the porch now. She would have looked like a deer in headlights if it weren't for the fact that she was still walking forward. Kipp moved in time to partly avoid the next blow, but it caught her on the elbow, sending pain reverberating through her gunshot wound. Instinctively, she clutched the throbbing spot, giving the man time to try another hit. This one landed on Kipp's stomach, causing her to keel over to the side and trip over her own feet.

"Go away! I'm going to call the police!" Morgan yelled from her position up the sidewalk.

He began sprinting towards her instead.

"No!" Kipp shrieked, shoving herself off the ground and running after him.

Morgan froze, her grip on the knife tightening.

Kipp leaned forward as she ran, hoping it would help her go faster. The man swung at Morgan sooner than she thought he would. The crowbar hit her hands and the knife went clattering onto the sidewalk.

"Stop!" Kipp screamed as the man lifted the crowbar. Morgan stepped back, throwing her arms up to defend herself from the incoming blow. The first hit her arm, but she couldn't move fast enough to block the one heading for the very top of her head. She collapsed on the sidewalk, unconscious. The man was preparing another swing when Kipp finally pounced on him.

Morgan's eyes cracked open a few minutes later. She felt a searing pain on the left side of her stomach, and her head throbbed like tiny explosions were going off inside. Her vision refused to focus no matter how hard she squinted. She could hear something, but the ringing in her ears muffled it.

Something appeared over her. It was a person, she could tell that much. Her movements were sluggish, but she managed to cross her arms over her face, hoping to avoid further injury.

"Hey, it's okay. It's just me. I'm here." Kipp carefully lifted Morgan's head off the sidewalk to rest in her lap.

Arms falling to her sides, Morgan let out some mixture between a whimper and a pained groan in reaction to another bout of pain shooting through her torso as she tried to sit up. "The ambulance is on its way. Just hang on." Morgan felt Kipp move her hands to squeeze the left side of her stomach. "You're going to be fine," Kipp assured.

Morgan's breaths were shallow, and she had to grit her teeth and squeeze her hands into fists to deal with the pain.

A bit of blood dripped from Kipp's nose onto Morgan's forehead. "Ah, sorry," she whispered, wiping it away with the sleeve of her blazer. Morgan's eyes briefly wandered to the man lying halfway on the sidewalk and halfway on the grass, unmoving and silent. She thought she could see some red staining his chest, but Kipp shifted, blocking her view. "Morgan, can you tell me where Amelia is?" she asked, starting to hear sirens in the distance.

"Working late," Morgan slurred after a moment.

"I'll call her, she can meet us at the hospital."

The ambulances came to a stop on the road in front of them, the back doors flying open. Two police cars parked behind it.

Morgan squinted at the bright white and red flashing lights, trying to make out what Kipp and the paramedic were saying.

"Is she bleeding?" the paramedic asked.

"Yes," said Kipp. Morgan looked down at herself, finally noticing the red staining Kipp's hands where they were clamped onto her side.

Some officers got out of the police cars and walked over to Kipp. Morgan could only make out parts of what Kipp was saying:

"...got the crowbar away from him… grabbed the knife… couldn't get there… stabbed her… knocked him over…trying to get it back… I stabbed him."

Morgan's eyes snapped all the way open at that last part. Kipp's hands on her stomach were soon replaced by a paramedic's, who started packing gauze into the wound. "Can you tell me your name?" the paramedic asked.

"Morgan Toner," Morgan responded as best she could. Her tongue felt thick and lifeless, and her words came out like molasses.

"Are you in any pain other than your stomach?"

"My head."

"And can you tell me the phone number of one or both of your parents?"

Kipp stepped in to tell her Amelia's phone

number. After she'd finished, the paramedic pulled a stretcher out of the ambulance. "Okay, Morgan, we're going to get you to the hospital." The woman looked up. "What's your name?" "Kipp Green."

"And are you in any major pain?"

"Not really. My nose might be broken though." Kipp took a step back, looking toward the ambulance. The man was being lifted inside, seemingly still alive judging by the lack of a body bag or sheet covering him.

"I'm going to need your phone number so that the department can contact you for another interview. How old are you?"

"Eighteen. Do you want my mom's phone number too?"

"That would be helpful in case we can't reach you."

Kipp gave the numbers and turned to walk to her car, but a small voice caused her attention to snap back to Morgan.

"Don't go," Morgan croaked. "Please?" She weakly reached out to Kipp as she was lifted onto the stretcher. The blood that had seeped into her black dress was almost unnoticeable. Her furrowed brow relaxed a bit when Kipp gingerly took her hand, tracing her thumb over it, but making sure not to aggravate the blooming bruises.

"Can I ride with you?" Kipp asked, turning back to

the EMTs lifting Morgan into the other ambulance.

"No, you'll have to drive separately behind us. We can get you some care for your nose when you get to the hospital. You can park right outside, tell them who you're there to see and they'll valet your car."

"Got it." Kipp nodded once.

"I thought I'd kill him by accident. I'm sorry," said Morgan.

"Don't worry about it," she said, taking her girlfriend's hand again.

"No, I could've helped. Are you okay?" Morgan asked, her words still bleeding together.

"I'm fine. You need to relax. I'll meet you at the hospital."

"No, please stay," Morgan pleaded, her grip weakly tightening on Kipp's hand as tears gathered in her eyes.

"You'll see her there, don't worry," the paramedic said, prying Morgan's hand off and motioning for Kipp to move away. With one last look at Morgan, Kipp rushed to her car and started the engine. As the ambulance sped forward, she took a quick breath and went after it. She let the car careen around corners and speed past other vehicles; all the while, her eyes were trained on the white and blue van in front of her. Sirens from the ambulance blared in her ears, but she didn't mind, only kept her hands glued to the steering wheel, which was becoming slick from her clammy hands.

As the ambulance was approaching an intersection, Kipp could see the light was red. The ambulance sped through, and she almost pressed her foot on the brake, but pulled it back as the light miraculously turned green right as she got to the line. Suddenly, a car sped through the intersection, missing her by a few feet. Kipp slammed on the brakes, her nose almost hitting the steering wheel.

She couldn't get her mind to form any coherent thoughts as she started to hyperventilate, gasping in breaths as if she'd nearly drowned. Not being able to slow her breathing was making everything so much worse. No one knew she was on this random road headed to the hospital. What if she passed out and hit someone? Or if someone hit her? She was crying now. She thought she could hear someone honking behind her.

Gripping the steering wheel, Kipp looked up, watching as the ambulance began to fade into the distance. *No.* Without a second thought, she stomped her foot down on the gas pedal. The car lurched forward. Kipp zoomed down the road, taking every chance she got to move through lanes and past other cars, slowly making her way closer to the ambulance as she took increasingly slower breaths. Finally, she saw a road sign for the hospital in the near distance. The ambulance turned in, and Kipp followed. She was quick to yank the wheel, turning the car toward the entrance, where she stopped next to a security guard.

"Morgan Toner," she said on an exhalation through the shattered window, "I'm here to see Morgan Toner. What room will she be in?"

"You're going to have to stay in the waiting room. Someone will let you know when you can see her. In the meantime, you might want to get checked out," said the valet, gesturing to her bloody nose. Kipp sighed as she nodded, pulling away to park the car.

She took the slowest breaths she could, wiping the last of her tears away before walking in. She approached the front desk with an expression as close to a smile as she could.

"Hi. I was in an altercation and I'm here to see Morgan Toner, but I think I need some stuff, you know, fixed before that, because I think my nose is broken. I got hit in the face with a crowbar." She found herself letting out a small laugh.

The receptionist's brow furrowed as she began tapping her blue acrylic nails on the keyboard. "Okay then, if you'll just take a seat, we'll get you fixed up as soon as we can. It's probably going to be a *very* long wait, though."

"How long do you think it'll be?"

"Maybe ten hours? Could be up to twelve. You might be better off coming back in the morning."

"That's okay. If something happened with Morgan I'd want to be here."

As soon as Kipp sat down, she called her mom.

Roberta was frantic as Kipp told her what had happened. Within fifteen minutes, Roberta had rushed down to the hospital. She and Kipp sat together as they prepared for the long wait ahead. A while later, Sergeant Carson burst through the front doors. She talked with the receptionist for a while, and eventually made her way to the waiting room. When she spotted Kipp and Roberta, her tense expression turned into a tired smile. She went to sit beside them.

"Did they have any updates on Morgan?" Kipp asked.

"She's in the middle of some big procedure. The front desk worker said they don't know when she's going to be done." The sergeant sighed.

The waiting area was relatively quiet for a while. Kipp put on her headphones as a baby began to cry, holding her phone in her lap as she began watching a random show. Occasionally, a nurse would come out to inform someone of what condition their friend or family member was in, sometimes people's reactions were tears of relief, others were wails of anguish. A strain began to pulse in Kipp's neck, prompting her to hold the phone out in front of her, which quickly tired her arms. She leaned to one side of the seat as someone near her began coughing, a wet sound that made her want to cover her face with her shirt. Her head twitched toward the door every time it opened, hoping the person coming though would have news that Morgan would be fine. Two seasons into the show she'd started and frequent moments of dozing off, Kipp's mind was getting more clouded by the second. It felt as if her eyelids had weights attached to them. The pain in her nose had gone down, but the throbbing in her elbow persisted. She didn't know at what time she drifted off, but she woke up to her mom gently shaking her shoulder.

"Kipp, they're ready for you."

Kipp barely saw the nurse that guided her into the exam room. She droned out answers to the doctor's questions, and inhaled when he told her to, and when he manually relocated her nose, the stab of pain barely registered. Soon she was back in the waiting room, a painkiller prescription in her numb fingers, still waiting for an update on Morgan, and terrified of falling asleep again.

Eventually, a nurse walked out.

"Who is here to see Morgan Toner?" the woman asked from the front of the room. Kipp and Amelia stood up, the nurse acknowledging them and walking over.

"So before I get into any fine details, Morgan is going to be fine. Her intestines were punctured and we had to stitch it back up, so she'll have to take some antibiotics for a while." She handed Amelia an orange bottle. "Have her take one pill twice a day. She's awake right now and you'll be able to come see her. Keep in mind she'll still feel a little loopy from the anesthesia."

Everyone filed into the room where Morgan was sitting up in the starkly white hospital bed. Her face immediately lit up with a smile upon seeing her visitors.

"How are you feeling?" asked Amelia.

"A lot better than before. They gave me some painkillers. Is your nose okay?" Morgan asked, noticing the white bandages on the bridge of Kipp's nose.

"Yeah. It was a little out of place, but the doctor put it back," said Kipp.

"Did it hurt?" asked Morgan.

"Probably nowhere near how much that hurt," Kipp said, pointing to Morgan's stomach where stitches were hidden under her hospital gown.

"I guess that's true."

Kipp leaned in to lightly wrap her arms around Morgan.

Morgan was discharged, and after some help changing clothes, she was taken to the parking lot in a wheelchair. Roberta allowed Kipp to ride with Morgan and Amelia to help Morgan get settled in. Despite Kipp aching in numerous places, she was so at ease holding Morgan's hand in the car, that she couldn't even feel it.

They arrived at Amelia's house, Morgan settling at the kitchen table while Kipp immediately took out her pill bottle and shook one tablet into her hand.

She popped it into her mouth and stuck her head under the faucet, swallowing it down with the water.

"Hopefully this'll help a little," she said, sitting down at the table.

"Hopefully," Morgan replied. "Um, do you want to do anything? We could play a board game or cards, or go to my room. There's a TV in there. You don't have to stay, though. If you want to go back to your house, that's fine too."

"No, I want to stay. I'm not really in the mood for a game, but TV sounds good."

"Okay. My room is down here." She pointed down a hallway and began to walk, Kipp

following behind her.

As the opening vocals to *The Lion King* filled the room, Kipp laid back against the decorative pillows with both hands behind her head. After setting the remote on the bedside table, Morgan propped a pillow on the headboard to lean against.

Once in a while, she would glance over at Kipp, whose eyes never left the screen. As Simba was walking into the elephant graveyard, Kipp shifted to sit up with her back against the headboard. Morgan turned to look at her. Kipp responded by giving her a quick smile and turning right back to the screen. With no more glances, Morgan looked back at the movie. She heard the covers shifting again, although this time it was followed by arms wrapping around her.

"I'm really sorry this happened. There were some way smarter moves I could've made back there. I don't even know what I would've done if you didn't make it. I'm so sorry," Kipp murmured into Morgan's hair.

"Please don't blame yourself for this," Morgan whispered.

"I should've stayed with you. I could've grabbed the knife and kept the crowbar to keep that guy away, but I left you alone with him to throw the stupid crowbar away. That knife was on the ground right next to him. I basically invited him to stab you," Kipp lamented, a shaky sound that betrayed the tears in her eyes even as they were blocked from Morgan's vision.

"But you called an ambulance, and you held the wound closed until they got there. You drove to the hospital and waited hours for me to get out. And you're here right now. You've done enough." Morgan's hands joined together behind Kipp's back.

"I guess," Kipp relented, hugging Morgan tighter.

Morgan pulled away to look at Kipp. "What happened when I was unconscious? I remember seeing that man lying on the ground with blood on him. It might've been mine, but I thought I heard you say something about stabbing him."

"Yeah, that wasn't your blood on him. I couldn't get there before he stabbed you, and it looked like he was going to do it again, so I tackled him. When he kept reaching for the knife, I grabbed it." Kipp let out a shaky breath, looking down at her hands. "I was afraid he'd keep trying to get the knife, or go grab the crowbar and… I stabbed him."

Morgan swallowed. "Did the police… Were they… understanding?"

"They didn't say anything about me needing to come in for questioning, so I think I'm in the clear."

"Are you sure?" she pushed, voice becoming high pitched and fast. "Did you tell them everything you told me? About him reaching for the knife? If you missed that, they might think you did it unnecessarily, and then if your fingerprints were on the knife they could even argue that you were the one that stabbed me—"

"I don't think that's going to happen. You can relax. We have both of us as witnesses and I don't think that guy was in his right mind. Trust me, they won't arrest me for anything."

"But what if they do?"

"They won't." Kipp put her hand on Morgan's shoulder.

Morgan let her head fall against Kipp's chest. "Please be right."

They stood there a while, unmoving. Morgan held onto Kipp as if she'd disappear if she let go. Although she knew it was unlikely Kipp would go to jail, especially with so much evidence against that man and an actual support system from friends and family, she couldn't tear her thoughts away from the image of Kipp being hauled off in a police car. She couldn't believe everything that had happened. It was like every time her life was close to becoming even a little bit normal, that hope was ripped away again.

"Kipp?" she said.

"Yeah?"

"Do you think it's possible to live normally after this?"

"Probably not. I mean, not completely normally as if this never happened, at least." Kipp gave a small shrug. "But I think the trauma that comes with stuff like this can lessen after a while. It'll probably be easier to get over when we have each other to relate to. We're also so much more badass now, so there's that."

Morgan exhaled through her nose. "There's that."

After a few days of diligently taking antibiotics, Morgan felt much better, and decided she should be the one to invite Kipp on a date for once. She called to ask Kipp out to dinner at a restaurant in Denver that Amelia recommended. They were seated at a small table by the window, under a low hanging light. Quiet chatter filled the dim room as Morgan and Kipp sipped on waters, deciding what to order.

"Amelia said this place has very good ribeyes,"

Morgan said, looking up from her menu.

"That's what I was thinking about getting. I'm excited to try it! Thanks for bringing me here."

"I thought it was probably time I invited you out somewhere instead of you taking me out, or asking me where I wanted to go and me trying to decide on something for hours." She laughed, setting her menu down. "I'm going to go to the bathroom." Morgan stood up, turning to start walking to the back of the restaurant. Suddenly, she felt her limbs turn to lead, threatening to pull her to the floor.

Kipp looked up from her menu. "Are you okay?"

Morgan didn't answer, but continued to stare, scrutinizing the face she had picked out from the many tables, trying to see if her eyes were playing tricks on her. They weren't. Everything was the same: the dirty blonde hair, the nose that always looked as if it was stuck up, the laughter that had become chilling to her.

"What is it?" Kipp asked, following Morgan's line of sight to two young women sitting at a table across the room.

"The blonde one. That's Grace. The one from my school."

"Holy shit. Want me to punch her for you?"

"No," Morgan laughed. Kipp's joke brought her back to the reality that Grace had lost the power she held over Morgan years ago. Morgan walked toward the bathrooms. She considered if she should do anything as Grace's table got closer.

Grace paused her conversation as she noticed Morgan approaching. She raised her eyebrows, looking Morgan up and down and stifling a giggle. Her smirk was much less menacing than it used to be. Now, it was more annoying than anything.

Morgan found herself smiling as she walked, and when she was close enough, she lifted her middle finger just high enough so Grace could see it. Then, she turned and walked down the hallway, not bothering to give Grace so much as another glance.

Morgan went home feeling unbelievably satisfied with the night. She decided tonight was the night she would figure out what to do with her old backpack. She had shoved it under her bed the day she moved in, which by now was over a month ago. It hadn't been touched since. Morgan hadn't even bothered to take it out of its plastic bag. She settled onto the floor, sitting crisscrossed to stare under the bed. The plastic crinkled as she slid it out of the darkness. She pulled the backpack out and set it on the ground, resting her head on her hand as she pondered what to do with it.

She decided on throwing it away, but not before emptying it out. She pulled out a few notebooks from school, a pencil case, and a calculator. Looking through the pockets, she didn't find much: only a stick of gum and a mini pack of tissues— that was, until she reached all the way into the front pocket. At the very bottom, she felt something. It was a yellow mechanical pencil. Memories flooding her, she ripped off the end of the pencil and turned it upside down to shake it.

Her heart leaped as a small paper fell out. She rushed to unfold it, nearly brought to tears upon seeing the phone number in faded Sharpie.

"Amelia!" Morgan called before she had even gotten out of her room.

"What?"

"Could I borrow your phone?"

"Sure, why?"

"I found a phone number that my friend from middle school gave me. I was going to see if I could call her."

Amelia handed Morgan the phone. "Did you just find it?"

"It was in my old backpack."

"Is this the friend you were telling me about a while ago? Serena?"

"Yes," she answered, already copying the number onto the keypad. Morgan held her breath as the phone rang. She exhaled as a voice came through the phone saying, "Your call has been forwarded to an automated voice messaging system."

"She didn't answer," said Morgan.

Amelia waved for her to keep the phone. "Call again. If she still doesn't answer, leave a message. She might think it's a spam call if you don't."

"Okay." Morgan called a second time, and this time, she left a message. "Hi. I'm trying to contact Serena Miller, so if that's you, please keep listening. This is Morgan Toner from middle school. I found the phone number you gave me before you moved, so, um, please call me back. I'd really like to talk to you again. Bye." She looked up as she ended the message. "Do you think she has the same number?"

"Probably. Even if she got a new phone, her information would be transferred over to it, so everything would stay the same."

"Will she listen to the message?"

"I think so. But we pretty much have infinite tries if she doesn't."

Morgan stood there a while, cradling the phone as she licked her lips and tapped her foot on the ground. She let out a quiet gasp as the phone buzzed, the number from the paper flashing on the screen. She picked up.

"Hello?"

"Morgan?" the voice she hadn't heard in so long answered.

"Yes. Hi. I was scared you wouldn't answer."

"I was scared I'd never get to hear from you again!" Serena's voice had matured, losing its child-like high pitch, but it was still so clearly hers. "How are you? And, where are you? About four years ago, I got my parents to take me to visit your house, but there was a For Sale sign up and no one there."

"I was put into foster care. I'm in Rundale now."

"Did you get taken away? Were your parents arrested or something?"

"No." Morgan pursed her lips, glancing to where Amelia was still standing. "They're gone. I'm with a great foster mom who's going to adopt me. She's a police sergeant."

"That's great! I'm going to have to come visit you! I'm so glad you called."

"Me too."

"Hey, I wanted to ask if you're okay. It seems like you have a great living situation now, but I know going through something like you did would mess me up pretty bad. So, are you okay?"

Morgan smiled, knowing she finally knew the answer. "Yes."

Epilogue

It was a refreshing change for Morgan to see a judge smile at her.

"I have reviewed the home study and petition. Everything seems to be in order. I'm pleased to say that you are now officially a family," said the judge. By that point, there wasn't a single person in the courtroom that wasn't smiling as clapping filled the room. The air was a few degrees warmer than anyone in attendance would have liked, not that any of them cared.

Morgan, now officially Morgan Carson, was buzzing with happiness. She threw her arms around her mother.

"I love you," Amelia said into her daughter's hair.

"I love you too," Morgan said back, shuddering a breath.

Among the people sitting in the pews were Kipp and Roberta, along with Serena, Nikki, Isabel, and Luke, who'd used some of their Spring Break to attend. Captain Brumbly had also decided to go, along with a few of Amelia's colleagues. Morgan was only a month from turning nineteen, and though she had lost her childhood to her parents and the training school, there was no way she was going to let that get in the way of celebrating.

Looking on at Morgan embracing her new mother, Kipp felt her eyes grow hot, but even as a tear finally started rolling down her face, she didn't bother to brush it away. Kipp was almost finished with her first year of college at University of Colorado, Denver. She came back to Rundale often to see her mother and Morgan. Once in a while, Amelia would drive Morgan over to see Kipp and they would get lunch or dinner and stay in Kipp's dorm for a while, watching movies or talking with some new friends Kipp had met. Morgan had ended up going to Colorado State University, wanting to stay close to her friends and family. She planned to become a child therapist.

As Kipp was leaving the courtroom, she saw an unfamiliar face. A girl who looked her age was walking to the door with the crowd.

"Hey," Kipp called. The girl turned around. "I don't think I know you. How do you know Morgan and Sergeant Carson?"

"Oh, I was friends with Morgan in middle school."

"Serena?" Kipp said slowly, waiting to see if the girl would correct her.

"Yeah! How do you know Morgan?"

"I'm her girlfriend."

Serena grinned. "Nice. I'm glad everything seems to be coming together for Morgan. She really deserves it."

Kipp smiled, looking at Morgan laughing with Amelia at the end of the room. "Yeah."

Amelia invited everyone back to her house for an after party. A small tent was set up in the backyard for refreshments, as well as a cooler with some drinks. As Morgan was digging through the ice for a soda, she saw two people approaching her out of the corner of her eye.

"Morgan," said Amelia. "I want you to meet my mom,"

"I've waited so long to meet you! I just flew in from Minneapolis," said the white-haired woman standing next to Amelia.

Morgan hadn't known her biological grandparents, and she was nervous she'd say something that would cause her new extended family to not like her. She just replied with a smile and "Nice to meet you."

"Amelia's told me a lot about you. You're a beautiful young lady. And very smart I hear."

"Yes, she is," said the sergeant.

Roberta brought out the cake. It was originally a birthday cake, but she'd scraped off "birthday" and used some old icing she found in the back of the pantry to replace it with "adoption" in scraggly cursive. Just for fun, Amelia dug some birthday candles out of a drawer and stuck a few into the cake. She and Morgan blew them out quickly to avoid getting wax all over the frosting, smiling as everyone clapped.

Although Morgan would have liked her adoption to be her final time in a courtroom, that wasn't the case. The man that stabbed her was going before a judge at the end of March, which was coming up fast. He had accepted the plea deal that was offered, since there was so much evidence against him for the attempted murder, assault, attempted robbery, and drug possession. Morgan and Kipp were set to attend. Amelia had told her that the name change would take a while to go through, so she'd probably be called 'Morgan Toner' in court.

The Thursday of the trial, they arrived at eleven a.m. and took their seats on uncushioned wood. The judge walked in after a few minutes, a long black coat flowing behind her.

"All rise, court is now in session," said the bailiff. "The honorable judge McDowell presiding." The judge, a black-haired woman that looked to be in her fifties, sat down.

The clerk cleared his throat. "Your Honor, we are ready to proceed with state versus Gibson."

"Your Honor, may I approach the bench?" asked

the district attorney. He stood up almost robotically, maintaining the perfect posture he had while sitting.

"Yes, you may."

"This is the plea transcript and court file for the case." The DA handed the papers to the judge, who read them over for a minute.

"I will now hear a factual basis from the state," the judge said when she set the papers down.

"Your Honor," the DA began, "if this case had gone to trial, the state's evidence would have shown that Mr. Gibson has proven himself to be a danger to others." He went on to explain what had happened, his final sentence being: "There is no doubt that Mr. Gibson had intent to harm, and succeeded."

"Thank you," said the judge. "I will now hear a factual basis from the defense."

The defense attorney cleared his throat, standing with a more fluid motion than the DA. He wore a navy suit with a tie that didn't quite match. "Your honor, had this case gone to trial, our evidence would have shown that this event was just as much the victims' fault as it was Mr. Gibbons's. That night, Mr. Gibson was under the influence of cocaine, something he had been struggling with for months. It was an especially addictive type, referred to as unicorn dust by the drug cartel that he bought it from."

Morgan and Kipp looked at each other. They could both tell what the other was thinking: *Hall's drugs.*

The defense attorney continued. "Although he threatened Miss Green with the crowbar, if she were to have given up her wallet and keys and then called the police, it's likely nothing that followed would have occurred."

Morgan felt a small pang of anger. Was he really choosing to blame Kipp for what happened?

"As the state said, Green proceeded to attempt to get the crowbar away from him. There was no way he could have known what she planned to do, had she succeeded. In his state of mind, to him, fighting to keep the weapon in his possession could very well have been an act of self defense."

Self defense. Morgan felt empathy begin to creep into her mind.

"Mr. Gibson eventually managed to get the crowbar away from Green and in order to prevent the authorities being called, incapacitated Miss Toner. When Miss Green managed to get the crowbar away from him, he was beginning to fear serious injury, so he made the regrettable decision to stab Miss Toner in hopes of distracting Green for long enough to escape. Then, rather than let him run off and run to the aid of Toner, Green decided to needlessly stab him instead."

"Thank you. I will now hear from the state on sentencing," said the judge.

"The state asks Your Honor to accept the deal as

tendered. If you are so inclined, the victims are here right now and would like to be heard," said the DA.

"Go ahead," said the judge. "What would you like to tell the court?"

Kipp stood up with the sheet of paper containing her statement.

"What happened that night was definitely an experience I'm not going to forget very soon. And most of it wouldn't have happened if he hadn't been involved." She glanced at Gibson with a face as cold and calm as a mountain lake. "This man tried to take someone's life, and someone who had so much life to live, no less. Morgan has so much left to do in life, I honestly don't know what I would've done if she didn't make it. I hope Mr. Gibson is truly remorseful for what he did, and truly understands the weight of what his actions could have resulted in. Thank you." Kipp sat back down, folding her hands on the table, and looked over at Morgan. They made eye contact as Morgan clutched her paper.

Morgan stood up to speak. Her heart was pumping blood as if it was preparing her body to sprint away at any given second. Maybe she should've warmed up her voice. That might have helped with the numbness spreading through her vocal chords.

"I, um—" Her voice cracked, and she stopped talking, half-contemplating whether she should just sit back down. She felt something warm curl around her hand. Looking down, she saw Kipp had taken hold of it, a small, reassuring smile on her face.

Morgan took a breath, words finally finding their way out of the maze that her mind had become in that moment. "I am grateful that the state is responsible for the medical bills from my injury, and I'm even more grateful to have survived. It takes a certain kind of person to kill another human being, whether they were broken down and pushed to by an outside force, or found joy and satisfaction in it. Having said that," she said, looking at the man, "I believe that people can change, but I think changing requires a full understanding of the weight of your actions and having remorse for them. That, and a lot of time.

"You are fortunate enough to go through the rest of your life without the shadow of my death looming over you. If you say you regret this, I hope that you mean it. I hope you get the help you need, and end up putting some good into this world." Her heart was still beating rapidly as she sat down, and her hands just barely shook as she folded her arms over her stomach. At first, she kept her eyes on the table, but eventually brought her gaze up to face the judge.

"Anything from the defense on sentencing?"

"Your Honor, Mr. Gibson was under the influence of drugs at the time. He woke up at the hospital with very little memory of what happened and was devastated when he learned of his actions. His family and friends can attest that he is normally never violent and has been working to fight his addiction. He was extremely cooperative with the investigation, and showed remorse throughout it," said the attorney.

The man then went to the stand to be questioned on his understanding of the agreement with questions that Morgan recognized all too well. Finally, the judge confirmed the sentence.

"I accept this plea deal. Mr. Gibson, you are sentenced to twenty years in state prison. Anything else the state would like to say?"

"No, your honor," said the DA.

"Anything on behalf of the defense?"

"The defense would like to ask the court to waive any court fees, as Mr. Gibson does not have a steady income source, and has been supporting his elderly mother for the past few months."

Morgan often wondered when it was appropriate to feel pity for people who hurt her. This man was going to prison for twenty years after hurting one person, while she'd served five after killing three. But it wasn't like she'd done it without reason. Each one was an awful mistake that she had mourned ever since. Maybe it was time to take a little pity from the dead and give it to the frail shell of a person she used to be.

Soon enough, Morgan and Kipp were walking out of the courtroom.

"You did great. I'm so proud of you." Amelia

stood up from the pews in the back when Morgan and Kipp started walking out. Morgan smiled.

"Do you guys want to get ice cream or something?" asked Kipp.

"I'd love some," Morgan replied.

"That sounds like a great idea. Do we need to wait for your mom? Is she here?" Amelia asked.

"No, she couldn't come. She really wanted to, but she was stressed over some work stuff and I told her she should just work on that," said Kipp.

"Aw. I hope she isn't too overworked."

"Yeah, she's just a little overwhelmed right now, but she works through it pretty quickly. Do you guys want to go to that ice cream place by the book store?"

"You two go ahead. I'll meet you at home." She gave Morgan a quick hug.

Kipp and Morgan drove over to the ice cream parlor, parking in a small parking lot beside the shop..

Kipp pushed open the door, immediately inhaling the scent of freshly made waffle cones.

The two ate their ice cream outside in the air quickly warming with the late day sun.

"I still don't understand how you can eat something that tastes like toothpaste with chocolate chips in it," Kipp said, side-eyeing Morgan's cone of mint chip.

"And I don't understand how your taste buds don't appreciate something like this," Morgan replied.

A soft laugh came from Kipp. "I guess mine

aren't as sophisticated as yours. Are you excited for college?"

"Yeah, I feel pretty prepared. How hard was it for you to make friends at college?"

"I mean, it's not that hard to at least get people interested in talking to me, when we do icebreakers in class and I say I was almost murdered by a drug lord. You could always strike up a conversation about that."

"That's true." Morgan smiled. "Speaking of that, I just started going to therapy. I like it more than I thought I would. Have you ever gone?"

"No. I don't think I need to, but my mom says I'm just being stubborn. I might try going to the counselor at school and see how it is talking to someone who will be able to dissect my brain about what's really going on with my feelings and stuff."

"Do you think about what happened a lot?"

Kipp paused, eyes flicking to the ground. "Every day. There's so many things that remind me of it. Like, I'll see an old building and I'll think, 'Huh, I wonder if there's a bunch of mobsters in there' or I'll get on my bike and ride over a bridge and be like, 'Wouldn't it be funny if I fell off like that one time?'"

"Yeah, I think about it a lot too. Especially the fact that we're one in a billion to have something like this happen to us. Everything, I mean. That's just insane to me, that all that could happen to two people."

"At least we got each other out of it."

"You have chocolate all over your mouth," Morgan said with something close to a smirk.

"Could you get it off for me?" Kipp couldn't suppress the grin that spread over her features.

Morgan rolled her eyes, still smiling as she leaned forward to wipe a napkin over Kipp's face. Only after the ice cream was gone from Kipp's mouth did Morgan lean far enough so that their lips could meet and savor the remaining sweetness.

Acknowledgements

Writing this book has been a blast. I've loved watching this piece change from a four-page, horribly written ramble session of a 6th grader, to the novel it's become! I have many people to thank for this evolution:

First off, I'd like to give a huge thanks to my editor and summer program teacher, Ríoghnach Robinson (aka Riley Redgate), who is the main reason this book was developed to the level it is. Riley, you were an amazing teacher at Interlochen, and made me not want to give up on this piece. Your guidance is a *massive* part of why this book is where it is now. I'll see you on Tumblr!

I would also like to thank my mom, Emma Astrike-Davis, Sabrina Garcia, Shannon Tucker, and Georgia Nixon who answered my many logistical questions. Julia Stivers also helped me out with a final check on the manuscript. Last but not least, Madelyn Worcholik helped me in the early stages of writing by encouraging me to really get to know the story I was writing. I am also very appreciative to the person who helped me take steps toward publishing: Matt Zemon. I am eternally grateful to each of these people. If this book was somehow published without them, I can assure it would have been of a much worse quality.

Lastly, if any readers decided to look at these acknowledgements, thank you! Your time put into reading this book means a lot, and I hope you enjoyed it!

Milton Keynes UK
Ingram Content Group UK Ltd.
UKHW012117271123
433389UK00003B/76

9 798989 305520